S0-AUD-029

英文

日本絵とき事典 9

ILLUSTRATED
WHO'S WHO OF JAPAN
100 HISTORICAL PERSONAGES

［人物日本史］

HAY LIBRARY
WESTERN WYOMING COMMUNITY COLLEGE

DISCARDED

ILLUSTRATED
WHO'S WHO OF JAPAN

© 1987 by Japan Travel Bureau, Inc.
All rights reserved

No part of this book may be reprinted in
any from without written permission
from the publisher, except by a reviewer
who may reproduce a few brief passages
and pictures from it.

First edition 1987

Printed in Japan

About this Book

1) Layout

Who's Who of Japan is comprised of the following four historical sections: 1) Ancient Times; 2) the Middle Ages; 3) the Pre-Modern Age; and 4) the Modern Age. In addition to historical sequence, this book may be read by looking up specific sections according to the names of historical figures of that time. Please refer to the name index at the back of the book. Many vocabulary entries not explained in the main text are marked with asterisks, with definitions presented in a glossary at the back of the book.

2) Japanese Words

All the Japanese words in this book have been romanized in accordance with the revised Hepburn system. Except for the names of places and people, all Japanese words are printed in italics except where they appear in headings or bold type. Long vowels are indicated by a line above, as in 'Syacho' and, since e's are pronounced "ay" in Japanese, e's at the ends of words are marked with an acute accent, as in 'shita-uké" (pronounced "shitahukay").

▓ Dear Readers ▓

Archaeologists have compiled firm proof that the Japanese archipelago has been occupied by human beings since the Old Stone Age. In terms of documentary records alone, Japanese history can be traced back more than 17 centuries, with this period representing a colorful saga of fierce and often cruel struggles for power, and the glory and tragedy of an unending stream of heroes.

This book presents a unique overview of the episodes and cultural legacy of the emperors, aristocrats, generals and statesmen who helped build the Japanese nation, as well as the artists and scholars who played key roles in the creation of Japan's distinctive art and culture.

It is our sincere hope that this brief taste of Japanese history will foster understanding of how Japan developed to its current position in the world order, and encourage further reading on this vast and stimulating subject.

CONTENTS

THE PRE-MODERN AGE 近世

THE MODERN AGE 近代

ANCIENT TIMES

◄‖古代‖►

ANCIENT TIMES

The history of Japan can be traced as far back as the Stone Age. As the native inhabitants became capable of agricultural pursuit, rice-paddy farming spread throughout the islands, leading to the formation of communal living. This gradually prompted the appearance of the first real governing power, a development generally considered to date from around the first century B.C. from the third to fourth century A.D., Japan was unified by the *Yamato* Court, the distant ancestors of the present Imperial family, with the islands at last brought under control as a nation state.

A government organization with the Emperor as its focus was established in the Asuka period (593 – 710), and reached its peak during the Nara period (710 – 794). In the Heian period which followed (794 – 1192), powerful nobles with vast land holdings in the outlying regions rose to the fore, and began to seize the reigns of control. In this way, while the gaudy age of aristocratic culture (with the Imperial Court at its core) flourished in all its splendor, conditions in the regions grew chaotic, with a marked increase in robber barons and revolt shaking the very foundation of the government. Toward the end of the Heian period, border guards were organized to protect the fiefs of the aristocrats, leading to the formation of Japan's warrior *(samurai)* class. Under the prevailing tone of social unrest, the *samurai* soon rose to positions of considerable power, bringing to a close more than eight centuries of Imperial rule.

In the spiritual realm, meanwhile, Buddhism entered Japan from the Korean peninsula from about 538, with the rapid increase in adherents leading to its establishment as a state religion from the seventh century on. Buddhist beliefs continue to wield a heavy influence on the thinking and behavior of the Japanese people today.

HIMIKO
卑弥呼・around 3rd century

Queen of third-century Japan which was not yet a unified nation, Himiko ruled *Yamatai-koku* and many smaller countries surrounding it. According to traditional belief, *Yamatai-koku* was a considerably powerful country, dispatching a mission to the Emperor of the Wei (China), who recognized Himiko as the sovereign of Japan. Nevertheless, the locality of *Yamatai-koku* has not been confirmed to date. Excepting some ancient Chinese records, no authentic literature about Himiko is available today. Thus, her life is shrouded in sheer mystery.

Legend has it that Himiko lived in a huge, fenced palace under strict guard of soldiers. She was a living god, and no one, except for her younger brother, could even get a glimpse of her figure.

Yayoi period

In the days of Himiko, people were living in poor dwellings dug in the ground, with rice cultivation as the main source of their livelihood. Today we can tell part of their lifestyle by examining earthenware of the Yayoi period, the decorative patterns on which consist entirely of delicate lines.

Earthenware of the Yayoi period

12

Himiko's place

It is believed that Himiko was a sort of witch, or prophetess. According to traditional belief, Himiko employed as many as a thousand maids in her palace, but she stayed in the innermost part of the palace, never to shown herself in public.

Emperor of the Wei

Himiko was given the title of *"Shingi Waō"* (king of Japan, Vassal of Wei) by the Emperor of the Wei, whereby she ruled *Yamatai-koku* and surrounding countries. However, whether or not *Yamatai-koku* had anything to do with *Yamato Chōtei,* which was to unite separate countries into a single state, has yet to be verified.

Sakaki

Miror

Red sash

White dress

Legend has it that whenever Himiko delivered an oracle, she was attired in white, with the sleeves tucked up with a red sash, adorned herself with jewels from head to foot, and danced about crazily, with a copper mirror hung from her neck and a branch of *sakaki* (sacred tree) in her hands.

It is believed that when Himiko died, a huge mound of tomb, exceeding 100 meters in length, was built and more than 100 slaves were buried alive there, together with her body and such objects as mirrors, jewels, swords, and earthenwares. However, the location of this tomb has not been spotted.

Emperor *(Tennō)* of the *Yamato chōtei* (imperial court of ancient Japan). He devoted his reign to strengthening the foundation of his nation by introducing advanced culture and technology from the Korean peninsula, developing large tracts of farmland in various parts of the country, and so on. It is said that the name *"Nintoku"* (meaning virtue in Japanese) was given the Emperor posthumously by those who adored him for his virtue.

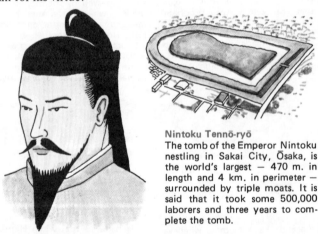

Nintoku Tennō-ryō
The tomb of the Emperor Nintoku nestling in Sakai City, Ōsaka, is the world's largest — 470 m. in length and 4 km. in perimeter — surrounded by triple moats. It is said that it took some 500,000 laborers and three years to complete the tomb.

Here's a story exemplifying the charitable character of the Emperor. One day he stood on a hill overlooking a small village, when he noticed that not a streak of smoke was rising from the chimneys of the village houses, while it was about time for evening meal. He then immediately made up his mind to exempt the villagers from taxes for the next three years because he thought that the villagers must have been so impoverished by heavy taxation that they could hardly afford even their evening meals.

Emperor of the Nara period. He was highly successful in consolidating the organization of the imperial court. Under his rule, pompous culture of aristocracy blossomed. On the other hand, a succession of struggles for political supremacy among the court nobles and Buddhist priests caused social uneasiness to mount. With a view to saving the situation with the help of Buddhism, the Emperor Shōmu endeavored to spread the religion by building Buddhist temples and monasteries throughout the country.

Shōsōin
Box of mother-of-pearl work — one of the best collections in the Shōsōin.

The reign of the Emperor Shōmu witnessed the apex of the *Tenpyō* culture characterized by overwhelming affect of T'ang (China). A wonderful collection of art objects of those days are well preserved in a treasury, the Shōsōin, at Nara.

Daibutsu
The lifework of the Emperor Shōmu was the building of *daibutsu* (Great Image of Buddha) of Tōdai-ji Temple, head of state-established provincial temples, at Nara. According to a legend, the Emperor himself, together with the laborers, carried buckets of soil in constructing the world's biggest image of Buddha.

SHŌTOKU TAISHI
聖徳太子・574—622

Great political figure of the Asuka period. Shōtoku Taishi is noted especially for having established the sovereignty of *Yamato Chōtei* which unified the state in the fourth century. There remain a variety of legends about Shōtoku Taishi who was generally considered a superman. Also, as a symbol of intelligence and virtue, he has long been an object of worship.

Shōtoku Taishi and his sons.

Yamashiro-no-Ōeno-Ōji

Eguri-ō

Hōryū-ji Temple
It is said that Hōryū-ji Temple at Ikaruga in Nara Prefecture was built by Shōtoku Taishi in 607. The original structure, however, was destroyed by fire, and the present one was built toward the end of the seventh century. Even so, the building is Japan's oldest temple having an air of the Asuka period.

Asuka period
During the period from the early sixth century till 645, the capital of *Yamato Chōtei* was in the Asuka district of Nara, hence the age is generally called the Asuka period. In the early part of this period, the ever intensifying struggles among powerful families in the locality were causing lots of bloodshed. Shōtoku Taishi put an end to the ferocious battles and did his best to establish a centralized government headed by the Emperor.

Legend of "Superhuman" Shōtoku Taishi

Kitashihimé

Image of Shōtoku Taishi
2 years old

One day *Kitashihimé*, who was to give birth to Shōtoku Taishi, had a dream of a priest of glittering gold. In her dream, the priest said to her, "I would like to borrow your womb for a while to save this chaotic world," then jumped into her mouth. Next morning, she found herself pregnant.

According to legend, it was in front of a stable that Shōtoku Taishi was born. On his birth, a reddish yellow light flashed around the garden. This reminds us of the birth of Jesus Christ in the stable. Thus, together with the Virgin Conception, the stories of the Old Testament transmitted to Japan via China must have contributed to the legend about the birth of Shōtoku Taishi.

In his childhood, Shōtoku Taishi had a quarrel with his brothers. Then, their father came along. At the sight of him, all the boys but for Shōtoku Taishi ran away. Asked why he didn't flee, Shōtoku Taishi answered, "I can't hide myself anywhere, so there's no alternative but to receive your punishment."

At the age of three, Shōtoku Taishi was asked which of the peach-blossom and pine-needle he preferred. His answer was 'pine-needle.' The reason he gave was that the peach-blossom would either soon, while the pine-needle would be evergreen.

17

At the age of 20, Shōtoku Taishi learned Buddhism from a high priest who came from the Korean peninsula. Many of the questions raised by Taishi could not be definitely answered even by that priest. Legend has it that one night Taishi had a dream of a gold-colored man appearing before him, and next morning he woke up to find that most of his questions had been solved.

When a Korean priest named Nichira met Shōtoku Taishi for the first time, he cried, "This child is a god!" and immediately knelt down with his hands joined. On that occasion, says the legend, Nichira emitted brilliant beams of light from all over the body just like he were wrapped in flames, and the light emitted from between Taishi's eyes were as glorious as the sun.

The intellect of Shōtoku Taishi was far greater than that of ordinary people. While he was administering the affairs of state as Sesshō* (regent) to the Emperor, he used to listen to ten statesmen talking utterly different things at the same time, and yet, he could always manage to comprehend their talks accurately and never made misjudgment.

Shōtoku Taishi's messenger

Emperor of the Sui

Shōtoku Taishi once sent an autograph letter to the king of the Sui Dynasty which was ruling China those days. In his letter, Taishi noted, "From the Emperor of the Land of the Rising Sun to the Emperor of the Land of the Setting Sun." At this, the king of the Sui grew angry, saying disgustedly that the letter from the barbarian was full of discourtesy and insolence.

The achievements of Shōtoku Taishi

Wallpainting in Hōryū-ji Temple

As a patron of Buddhism, Shōtoku Taishi made the religion the keynote of his government policies. As a result, a Buddhist culture called the Asuka culture flourished in and around the Asuka district in which the capital was located.

One of the greatest achievements of Shōtoku Taishi was the promulgation of the Constitution of Seventeen Articles. This was a code of administrative ethics for court officials, stating that the Emperor was the Heaven and his vassals were the ground; that since the master of the common people was the Emperor, no powerful family was allowed to collect any tax from them without permission of the Emperor; and so on. Thus, the constitution was a concise statement of Taishi's policy aiming at strengthening imperial power.

Buddhist images in Hōryū-ji Temple

Shōtoku Taishi in his later years

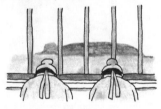

Toward the end of his life, Shōtoku Taishi used to keep to the temple all alone, conversing with Buddha. He eventually came to think that this world was a temporary one and the spiritual world after death was the real one. Thus he held religion as the only salvation for his soul.

In the winter of 612, Taishi's mother passed away. On *Shōgatsu* (New Year's Day) of the following year, Taishi and his wife fell ill. He died of the illness on February 22 of the same year, following his wife, who deceased on February 21. Taishi, his mother, and his wife lie in the same tomb in the grounds of Eifuku-ji Temple at Nara.

Poetry flourished immediately before the Nara period.
Kakinomoto-no-Hitomaro brought to perfection *Tanka*, a form
of Japanese poetry with five lines in a pattern of 5, 7, 5, 7, and
7 syllables having a unique rhythm. His bold, magnificent style
has never been challenged in this particular field of Japanese
literature. Some 100 of his poems are contained in Japan's first
anthology called the *Man-yōshū*. Although there remain many
legends about Hitomaro, little has been known about his life
and personality.

There is a monument describing a *tanka* of Hitomaro in Sakurai City, Nara Prefecture. Since Hitomaro visited various places in the western part of mainland Japan, there remain a good number of such monuments to him.

Man-yōshū

Anthology compiled toward the end of the eighth century. It contains a total of 4,500 poems, of which 4,200 are *tanka.* They can be largely divided into three categories: *sōmon* (love poems), *banka* (poems on the death of one's spouse, close friend, etc.), and *zōka* (miscellaneous poems). Besides Kakinomoto-no-Hitomaro, three poets are worth special mention: Yamanoué-no-Okura who composed contemplative poems; Yamabé-no-Akahito who had a passionate love for nature; and Ōtomo-no-Tabito who pursued the beautiful. The *Man-yōshū* is considered by many to be no less superb than the *Kokinshū* compiled in the Heian period, the *Shin-Kokinshū* of the Kamakura period, or any of several other excellent anthologies. As the foremost anthology of *tanka,* the *Man-yōshū* has long been loved by many Japanese.

Hyakunin Isshu — the Hundred Poems by One Hundred Poets

Hitomaro

Wife of the Emperor

The life of Hitomaro is shrouded in mystery — even the years of his birth and death are unknown. It seems the only certainty about him is that coming from good stock, he distinguished himself as an exceptionally talented poet from his youth.

Many of Hitomaro's *sōmon-ka* (love poems) are concerned with free and unrestrained love. According to legend, he was condemned to exile on the suspicion of illicit love with a wife of the Emperor.

Toward the end of his life, Hitomaro was sent to a desolate island off the shore of Shimané Prefecture. After he returned to the mainland, he wandered from place to place and died in Shimané. The poems Hitomaro composed in his last years are filled with his deep longing for the capital of Nara or his feeling of the uncertainty of life. These poems are generally considered the best of his works.

Hitomaro was deified after his death, probably because later people feared the curse of the revengeful ghost of Hitomaro who died a tragic death in a spell of bad luck as Sugawara-no-Michizané (see p.22) did.

SUGAWARA-NO-MICHIZANÉ
菅原道真・845—903

Renowned scholar of the early Heian period*. Taken into government service by the Emperor, Sugawara-no-Michizané was eventually promoted up to *Udaijin* (one of the two top advisers to the Emperor) at the age of 54. He was then deceived by his political rival, Fujiwara-no-Tokihira, and relegated to Kyūshū. He died of an illness in distress there.

Raijin

Demoted to a mere local official of a district far away from the capital, Sugawara-no-Michizané conveyed his homesickness and innocence in highbrow poems in Japanese or Chinese. However, he was never allowed to return permanently to the capital.

After the death of Sugawara-no-Michizané, the Seiryō-den Palace, the Emperor's residence, was often struck by lightning. People thought this was the vengeance by the dead Michizané reincarnated into *Raijin* (God of Lightning).

Kitano Tenman-gū Shrine

It is Kitano Tenman-gū Shrine at Kyoto that was built to appease the vindictive spirit of Michizané. Originally a scholar, Michizané came to be revered as a god of learning. Today the Shrine is visited by many students preparing for an examination to pray for good luck.

Military commander of the middle Heian period. A member of a powerful family in the Kanto district (area around present-day Tokyo), Taira-no-Masakado was noted for bravery. Rebelling against the imperial court, he brought the greater part of the Kantō district under his control by the sword and professed himself to be *Shinnō* (new Emperor). However, he died in a surprise attack staged by another powerful family in the locality.

Tomb of Masakado at Ōtemachi in Tokyo

Masakado's Head Mound

In the Kanto district, there are a number of mounds in which, as legend has it, Masakado's head was embedded. Incidentally, the Kanda-Myōjin, one of the most popular shrines in Tokyo, is dedicated to Masakado.

There are several versions of legend about the head mound. According to one version, the head mound is the place on which Masakado's head that had whirled up from its pillory landed. Another version has it that the head mound is the spot at which the body of Masakado with his head chopped off fell after a long dash from the place of execution.

The most prominent man of power of the Heian period.
Coming of noble stock, Fujiwara-no-Michinaga rose to *Udaijin**
at the age of 30. Then, he expelled all his political rivals in succession, got one of his daughters to marry the Emperor, and
finally, succeeded in having his grandson ascend the throne.
Michinaga remained in *Sesshō Kampaku*(the highest post of regency) for as many as 21 years. During that period, the Fujiwara family lived in unparalleled splendor.

Fujiwara-no-Michinaga

Eldest daughter

‖
Emperor Ichijō

Second daughter
‖
Emperor Sanjō

Third daughter = Emperor Go-ichijō

Matrimonial relations of Fujiwara family

In the aristocracy of the Heian period, establishing close matrimonial
relations with the imperial family was the shortest way to political supremacy. Michinaga got his eldest daughter to marry Emperor Ichijō, and
his second daughter to marry Emperor Sanjō. Then, he had his grandson
(the son between his first daughter and Emperor Ichijō) ascend the
throne as Emperor Goichijō. After that, Michinaga got his third daughter to marry Emperor Goichijō (Michinaga's grandson). Thus, by marry-
ing his daughters into the imperial family in successive generations,
Michinaga firmly gripped undisputed political power. In those days, not
a few emperors ascended the throne in their teens and retired in their
twenties. This made it easier for Michinaga, the Regent, to wield political power in his own way.

Michinaga was apparently aggressive and self-confident by nature. Here's a legend attesting to it.

One day, Michinaga's father sighed before his children, saying "My cousin Yoritada has a clever son named Kinto. You, dull fellows, won't even be able to step on the shadow of Kinto." To this, Michinaga responded saying, "I won't step on his shadows. Rather, I'll stamp down his face."

When Michinaga was 30, the measles ranged fiercely around the capital, claiming the lives of eight high-ranking court nobles out of fourteen. Owing, at least partly, to this happening, Michinaga could rise to an important post in government.

Hō-ō-dō:main hall of Byōdō-in Temple

When Michinaga was 53, the marriage between the Emperor Goichijō (Michinaga's grandson) and Ishi (Michinaga's third daughter) was celebrated at the apex of Fujiwara power. At the banquet, Michinaga improvised a noted poem to the effect that his power was like a full moon lacking nothing in any respect and hence he was often tempted to think this world was his.

Michinaga spent his later years praying to Buddha in a gorgeous temple called Byōdō-in Temple which he had built hoping that he could gain admission into *Jōdo* (Buddhist heaven) after his death. Legend has it that when he died of illness at the age of 62, a string extending from the statue of *Amida-Nyorai* (the Buddha believed to guide the dead to *Jōdo*) was gripped firmly in his hands.

25

SEI SHŌNAGON
清少納言・966—1025

In the history of Japanese literature, the Heian period was the golden age of literary works written by women. Sei Shōnagon, famous for her witty essays *"Makura-no-Sōshi,"* was one of the most prominent woman writers of this period. Sei Shōnagon was a *nyōbō* (court-lady) who served Teishi, one of the empresses of the Emperor Ichijō. Thus, her work *("Makura-no-Sōshi")* provides the reader with a vivid description of the life of her contemporary court nobles.

Makimono

In those days, literary works were written on *makimono* (rolls of long strip of Japanese paper) using ink and brush. They were spread among the noble society by reading aloud or *shahon* (transcription).

Literary woman of the Heian period

Most of the emperors of the Heian period normally had two legal wives titled *Kōgō* (Empress) and *Chūgū* (second imperial consort), respectively, and a considerable number of other consorts titled *Hi, Fūjin, Hin, Nyōgo* etc. The residence of these wives and *Nyōbō* serving them was called *Kōkyū*. Since the emperor's wives vied with one another in recruiting talented women as their *nyōbō*, much of the cultural splendor of the Heian period originated in *Kōkyū*.

In *Makura-no-Sōshi,* Sei Shōnagon writes as follows: "Happily exciting to me are watching a young sparrow hopping toward me with unsteady steps, idly lying on *tatami* (straw mat) alone with incense burning, and secretly looking in a mirror in a dark room."

According to traditional belief, Sei Shōnagon was self-confident and unbending, often avowing that she could not stand coming out second best to others in anything. As a matter of fact, *Makura-no-Sōshi* contains a lot of her brags.

On a snow evening, Teishi asked Sei Shōnagon what the snow on the Kōrohō (a mountain in China) was like. Remembering the famous paragraph "I raise the rattan blind and see the snow of Kōrohō" in a popular Chinese poem, Sei Shōnagon wound up the bamboo blind and showed Teishi the snow lying on the ground. Such a game to test the level of the companion's culture seems to have been very popular among the court nobles.

MURASAKI SHIKIBU
紫式部・980—1014

The exceptionally long novel *"Genji Monogatari"* written by Murasaki Shikibu is not only the foremost literary work of the Heian period. It is also one of the supreme glories of Japanese literature. This classical work which describes, in high-flown style, an amazingly eventful life of an intelligent, handsome noble *"Hikaru Genji"* is even today admired by many Japanese readers.

Combination of Hiragana and Chinese character

Murasaki Shikibu was a *nyōbō* (court-lady) who served Shōshi, wife of the Emperor Ichijō. She was a contemporary of Sei Shōnagon. In striking contrast with Sei Shōnagon who went to everything showy, Murasaki Shikibu liked to be reserved in the presence of others. So it seems that she disliked Sei Shōnagon. In her diary, Murasaki Shikibu notes: "She (Sei Shōnagon) is a disgusting woman, looking big. Sooner or later, she will give herself away, only to learn a lesson."

The characteristic woman literature of the Heian period was made possible partly by the invention of *hiragana*, a Japanese syllabary. While Chinese characters were officially used in those days, the use of *hiragana* in combination with Chinese characters dramatically increased the breadth and depth of presentation. *Hiragana* were formerly called female characters, and in the Heian period they were used only by women.

Plot of Genji Monogatari

Hikaru Genji, hero of the novel, was born between an emperor and his low-ranking wife. He is described as a perfect man gifted with good looks, talent, and noble character. *Genji Monogatari* is a story describing extravagant, yet repentant, love affairs of Hikaru Genji with his many lovers.

The first lady whom Hikaru Genji loved was Kiritsubo who had much of the image of his mother. Kiritsubo was another wife of his father, or a mother-in-law of Hikaru Genji. Thus the story begins with the illicit love of Hikaru Genji with Kiritsubo.

While Hikaru Genji experiences love affairs with many noble beauties in succession, he can never forget his first lover Kiritsubo. Every one of the ladies falling in love with him becomes heartbroken, and none of them, including Hikaru Genji himself, feels happy for long.

Although Hikaru Genji is once relegated to an office in a remote place, he eventually returns to the capital of *Heian* (Kyoto), where he wins speedy promotion and lives a life full of splendor. It is the period in which Hikaru Genji spends his happiest days.

However, in his latter years, Hikaru Genji is far from happy. One of his wives has an illicit love affair with a young man, giving birth to a boy, who is named Kaoru. Reflecting the illicit love with his mother-in-law in his youth, Hikaru Genji is battered by the hardness of the world and enters the priesthood.

KŪKAI
空海・774—835

One of the most notable Japanese Buddhist priests. Also called *Kōbō Daishi*. In his teens, he started ascetic exercises with a view to matering the secrets of esoteric Buddhism (a branch of Buddhism whose teachings are mystical and secret). At the age of 31, he crossed the sea to T'ang (China), where he assiduously studied the teachings of Buddhism. When Kūkai returned home, he won the confidence of the Emperor as one of the most respectable priests of the Heian period. Eventually, he founded the *Shingon-shū* sect of Buddhism.

Kūkai was also a master of *shodō* (the art of calligraphy). The Japanese expression *"Kōbō mo fudé no ayamari"* (literally, Kōbō Daishi wrote clumsy characters) is sometimes used to refer to a failure which no one expected to occur.

Some time after Kūkai returned home from China at the age of 33, he was entrusted by the Emperor with the task of praying for peace of the nation — actually the most important task of priests in those days. He opened a seminary for the Buddhist priesthood in Mount Kōya (in Wakayama Prefecture). In his later years, he visited various parts of the country to propagate his teachings. There still remain various legends about Kūkai around the country.

Supernatural-power Contest at Shinsen Garden

In the Heian period, two Buddhist temples — Tō-ji (East Temple) and Sai-ji (West Temple) — were sharing control of the religious world. There is an interesting legend that has grown up around the power struggle between the two temples. Envious of Kūkai for his fame as head of Tō-ji Temple, a priest named Shubin of Sai-ji Temple used a charm to entrap *Ryūjin* (an imaginary animal living in the celestial sphere and causing rainfall) in a jar, thereby causing an extensive drought.

Challenged by Shubin to a supernatural-power contest at Shinsen Garden, Kūkai dispelled the curse of Shubin and set the *Ryūjin* free to cause rain to fall.

Spring water

Kōbō Shimizu (Spring Water)
There was a village suffering a spell of dry weather. One day a priest made his appearance and asked a villager for a cup of water. The villager readily served valuable water to the traveling priest. As the priest left the village, he struck the ground with his stick. Then, fresh water sprang from the spot. When the villagers saw this, they shouted "That priest was *Kōbō Daishi.*" They then named the spring water *"Kōbō shimizu."*

Oh, no!

Sweet Potatoes Turned to Stones
A peasant was digging up sweet potatoes, when a priest came along and asked him for some of the sweet potatoes. The peasant refused to give any, shouting "Why should I give my valuable crop to a mendicant priest?" The priest prodded one of the sweet potatoes with his stick without saying anything. Then, all the sweet potatoes in the hands of the peasant immediately turned to stones. It is said that this priest must have been Kūkai.

SAICHŌ
最澄 · 767—822

High priest of the early Heian period, ranked with Kūkai. At the age of 37, he crossed over to T'ang (China), along with Kūkai and some other priests, and returned home the following year. Eventually, he founded the *Tendai-shū* sect, an esoteric branch of Buddhism. Since then, the Konponchūdō Hall (today, the main hall of Enryaku-ji Temple) built on Mount Hiei by Saichō has been a Mecca of esoteric Buddhism, visited by a great number of believers all the year round.

Konpon-chūdō Hall

The Konpon-chūdō Hall houses the statue of *Yakushi-nyorai* (disease-curing Buddha) which, according to traditional belief, was carved by Saichō himself.

Mount Hiei is located northeast of Kyoto. According to *eki* (Chinese divination), the term "northeast" implied *kimon* (place where demons gather). Saichō dared to build the Konpon-chūdō Hall at a site northeast of the imperial court when he was only 21. As the Hall was regarded as a temple to protect the imperial court from evils, Saichō was ranked among the high priests at a bound. It is said, however, that the later years of Saichō were tumultuous ones due to rivalries within the sect.

Esoteric Buddhism

Esoteric Buddhism spread by Kūkai and Saichō is a branch of Buddhism which teaches the believer to be assiduous in practicing austerities to become a living Buddha. Naturally, therefore, the method of discipline of esoteric Buddhism is not taught to ordinary people. Thus, it is said that the teachings of esoteric Buddhism can be understood only by those who have attained a high degree of priesthood. On the other hand, there is another branch of Buddhism called *kengyō,* the teachings of which can easily be understood by anyone.

In

Kitō (Prayer to Buddha)
Esoteric Buddhism preaches that the believer can unite with Buddha by reciting *shingon* (teachings of Buddha) with his fingers set in a specific position called *in,* and that once he successfully becomes a 'living Buddha,' he is endowed with supernatural power to dispel diseases and evils from people in trouble.

Mandala (Picture of the Buddhas)
Most temples of esoteric Buddhism display a mandala depicting *Dai-nichi-Nyorai* (main Buddha of the *Shingon-shu* sect) surrounded by several other Buddhas. It is said that the mandala represents the Buddhist world of perfect enlightenment.

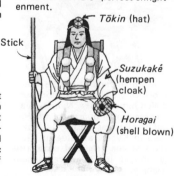

Tōkin (hat)

Stick

Suzukaké (hempen cloak)

Horagai (shell blown)

Yamabushi
Yamabushi is an esoteric Buddhist priest who led an ascetic life in the mountains, typically Mount Hiei. It was believed that *yamabushi* in resplendent costumes had mastered the secrets of esoteric Buddhism and were capable of working magic.

TAIRA-NO-KIYOMORI
平清盛・1118—1181

Supreme commander of the *Heishi* family, one of the leading military groups toward the end of the Heian period, Taira-no-Kiyomori was a notable historical figure symbolizing the turning point from aristocratic government to military government, or from ancient Japan to medieval Japan. Kiyomori who gained the reigns of government after winning the two decisive

The scroll with a superb picture on the front cover contains sutras written on paper which has gold and silver powder scattered on it.

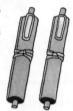

The Itsukushima Shrine in Hiroshima Prefecture, worshipped as a guardian deity by the *Heishi* family, displays a gorgeous *Kyōmon* (scroll of sutras) dedicated by the family. This scroll is one of few bequeathed articles reminiscent of the past glory of the *Heishi* family.

Torii (main gate)

Itsukushima Shrine

Toward the end of his life, Kiyomori entered the priesthood and called himself *Jokai Nyūdō*. Since the residential quarter of the *Heishi* family was located at Rokuhara in Kyoto, a statue of Kiyomori at the height of prosperity is housed in Rokuhara Mitsu-ji Temple.

battles of *Hogen* and *Heiji*, got one of his grandsons to ascend the throne, and thereby the *Heishi* family lived in splendor, boasting that nobody other than members of the *Heishi* family deserved the name. After the death of Kiyomori, however, the power of the *Heishi* family declined rapidly and the family perished soon after it was expelled from the capital of Heian by its mortal enemy — the *Genji* family. The rise and fall of the *Heishi* family in as short a period as 30 years is dramatically described in *Heiké Monogatari*, which is considered by many to be Japan's foremost historical romance.

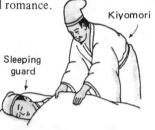

Kiyomori

Taira-no-Kiyomori was a very tender-hearted military commander respected by his vassals. According to legend, on severely cold winter nights, Kiyomori allowed his guards to rest in the skirts of his bedclothes, and on the next morning, when they were still asleep, he stole out his bed paying care not to awaken them.

Sleeping guard

The Civil War of Hogen (1156)

Toward the end of the Heian period, mounting political chaos in the face of the impotance of the aristocracy led to bloody civil wars for political supremacy. Kiyomori, on the Emperor's side, attacked the camp of the *Jōkō* army at night to frustrate their plot to overthrow the government. This civil war is called *Hogen-no-Ran*. The two powerful families, *Heishi* and *Genji*, which struggled through the war, eventually emerged to wage a contest for political power.

The Civil War of Heiji (1159)

Genji's red flag

Heiké's white flag

Discontented with the unusual promotion of Taira-no-Kiyomori, Minamoto-no-Yoshitomo of the *Genji* family attacked the Emperor and occupied the Imperial Palace while the *Heishi* army was away from the capital.

Returning to the capital, Kiyomori lured the *Genji* army away from the Imperial Palace and saved the Emperor from his confinement taking advantage of the enemy's unguarded moment. The *Genji* army came back to the Imperial Palace to find that the gates were closed tightly and a red flag—a symbol of the *Heishi* family—was fluttering high. Taira-no-Kiyomori thus defeated the *Genji* family, thereby holding undisputed political power firmly in his hands.

Glory days of Taira-no-Kiyomori

Taira-no-Kiyomori loved the lifestyle of the court nobles more than the nobles themselves. The *Heishi* family built sumptuous residences in Kyoto, and nobles visited Kiyomori with precious gifts for him. Many people thought that the *Heishi* family was above the Emperor in wealth and power.

Kiyomori was exceedingly delighted when his eldest daughter Tokuko married into the imperial family and gave birth to an imperial prince. Holding his grandson in his arms, Kiyomori would not let him go all day long. When the infant prince put his finger through a *shōji* (sliding paper screen) as instructed by Kiyomori, the grandfather was moved to tears and ordered an attendant to lock up that *shōji* deep in a warehouse. This prince was to become Emperor Antoku.

The fall of the Heishi family

Kiyomori died of an acute fever. According to an old document, he had a scorching fever all over the body, so a handful of snow placed on his forehead melted and turned to hot water immediately. The same document says that the doctor had to undress in order to take the temperature of his patient. It was rumored in the Heian capital that the fever of Kiyomori might be the evil consequence of the nobles and soldiers killed by him.

After the death of Kiyomori, the survivors of the *Heishi* family defeated by the *Genji* family began retreating westwards. Tokuko was also expelled from the capital. In a desperate situation, she threw herself into the sea, with the eight-year-old Emperor Antoku in her arms. However, her long hair floating on the sea was detected by a *Genji* soldier and she was pulled up from the sea, while her young son was sinking deep into the water. With their emperor lost, the *Heishi* family perished for good.

Heiké Monogatari

Heiké Monogatari, describing the rise and fall of the *Heishi* family, is a magnificent epic which was narrated by a blind *biwa* (lute) player called *biwa-hoshi*. Especially notable is its opening paragraph:

The bell of Gion Temple tolls into everyman's heart to warn him that all is vanity and evanescence. The fades flowers of the sala trees by the Buddha's deathbed bear witness to the truth that all who flourish are destined to decay.

ONO-NO-KOMACHI
小野小町・？ー？

Poetess and rare beauty of the early Heian period. Her private life (including the years of her birth and death) is shrouded in mystery. Tradition says that a young noble visited her one hundred consecutive nights to woo, but in vain. There are many legends exalting the beauty and talents of Ono-no-Komachi, but none of them is authentic.

Hyakusai-no-zō
Tōfuku-ji Temple in Kyōto houses two carved statues associated with Ono-no-Komachi. According to traditional belief, one of the statues, *Hyakusai-no-zō*, was modeled after a 100-year-old Ono-no-Komachi envisioned by herself. It might be that Ono-no-Komachi— a rare beauty—keenly felt that her exquisite looks would not last forever.

Tamazusa Jizō
The Tamazusa *jizō* (stone statue) has a cavity in the back, in which a good number of love letters delivered to Ono-no-Komachi are said to be hidden. Legend has it that Ono-no-Komachi remained unmarried, and childless, for life. The fact that there are many historic remains associated with Ono-no-Komachi in various parts of the country relates that her mysterious life, as well as her beauty, attracted attention of so many people.

THE MIDDLE AGES

◄‖ 中世 ‖►

THE MIDDLE AGES

The year 1192 marked the beginning of the Kamakura shogunate, Japan's fist full-fledged military government. For the nearly seven centuries from the Kamakura period (1192 – 1333) to the Meiji Restoration of 1867, true political power in Japan was consigned to the warrior class, with the *shogun* (generalissimo) at the helm.

In the late 13th century Japan was attacked twice by Mongol armies, and although the invaders were repelled both times, this marked the beginning of the decline of the Kamakura government. The chaotic times which followed witnessed an unsuccessful attempt by the Emperor to regain command of the nation, while in 1338 Takauji Ashikaga established Japan's second feudal military government – the Muromachi shogunate.

The Muromachi period (1338 – 1573) was characterized by a fierce rise in the power of regional *samurai,* with no lasting political stability achieved as a result. With an insurrection in 1467 the shogunate lost all real ability to rule, plunging the nation into an age of conflict between rival warlords. This war-shattered period from 1467 to the quasi-unification of Japan under Oda Nobunaga in 1572 is generally known as the Age of Warring States.

After Oda was betrayed by one of his henchmen and assassinated, Toyotomi Hideyoshi, one of Oda's close associates, took over the task of reuniting the nation, establishing a framework for an effective political state. After the death of Toyotomi, a fierce struggle between his forces and those of Tokugawa Ieyasu nearby spilit the nation in two. Tokugawa eventually prevailed, and with his foundation of the Edo shogunate Japan was at last firmly reunited, and instilled with the momentum to enter a new historical age. The rule of Oda and Toyotomi, which occurred during Japan's transition from its feudal to pre-modern age, is known as the Azuchi-Momoyama period (1572 – 1603). This age also marked the first visit to Japan by Christian missionaries, initiating contact between Japan and the West.

MINAMOTO-NO-YORITOMO
源頼朝・1147—1199

Founder of the Kamakura Shogunate*, Japan's first military government. Defeated in the battle of *Heiji*, Minamoto-no-Yoritomo was expelled from the Heian capital to Izu (in Shizuoka Prefecture) by Taira-no-Kiyomori of the *Heishi* family. However, in 1180, Yoritomo raised an army to put down the *Heishi* family, and eventually, with the aid of Minamoto-no-Yoshitsuné and his army, succeeded in annihilating the *Heishi* family.

Tōshō-gū Shrine at Nikkō is dedicated to Minamoto-no-Yoritomo, Toyotomi Hideyoshi (See p.78), and Tokugawa Ieyasu as "gods of *samurai* (warriors)."

Although Minamoto-no-Yoritomo was a man of outstanding political ability, he liquidated Minamoto-no-Yoshitsuné and his kinsmen in succession in order to maintain his power. Because of this, the *Genji* family lasted for only 20 years after the death of Yoritomo. Nevertheless, the fact that Yoritomo paved the way for the Shogunate to be later consolidated by Tokugawa Ieyasu (See p.92) and helped shift political power from the court aristocracy to the military class has great significance in Japanese history.

Ikenozenni

Yoritomo

When the battle of *Heiji* broke out, Yoritomo was only thirteen years of age. Brought before Tairano-Kiyomori as a prisoner, Yoritomo was almost killed on the spot. Through intercession of Kiyomori's mother Ikenozenni, Yoritomo escaped death and was eventually exiled to Izu.

Leading an army of some 300 soldiers, Yoritomo fought with a *Heishi* force ten times their numbers, and was defeated. Legend has it that a military commander of the *Heishi* family who had noticed Yoritomo hiding in a cave left him uncaught. This commander won rapid rise in Kamakura Shogunate.

The second time, Yoritomo commanding a great army of some 30,000 soldiers confronted a *Heishi* army across the Fuji river running through Shizuoka Prefecture. The commander-in-chief of the *Heishi* force was a coward, who on one night was frightened at the flapping of waterfowls and took to his heels back to Kyōto.

The tomb of Yoritomo at Kamakura (in Kanagawa Prefecture) is unexpectedly small in size.

As a *shogun* * (military dictator), Yoritomo died of a disease which originated in a wound he had received when thrown by his horse. Legend has it that the unnatural death of Yoritomo was caused by ghosts of the *Heishi* family ruined by him.

43

Military commander of the *Genji* family. According to traditional belief, Minamoto-no-Yoshitsuné was not only a genius in martial arts and a war hero carrying everything before him, but also an exceptionally handsome man. Despite the fact that Yoshitsuné played a leading part in beating the *Heishi* family, he died a violent death caused by his elder brother Minamoto-no-Yoritomo who was jealous of his brother's reputation. Thus, as a tragic hero, Yoshitsuné has long been very popular among the Japanese.

Gikei-do Shrine

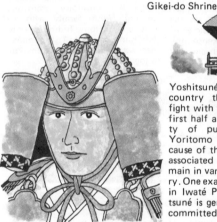

Yoshitsuné moved all over the country throughout his life—to fight with the *Heishi* family in the first half and to flee from the party of pursuers dispatched by Yoritomo in the second half. Because of this, many historic relics associated with Yoshitsuné remain in various parts of the country. One example is Gikei-dō Shrine in Iwaté Prefecture where Yoshitsuné is generally believed to have committed suicide.

The unusually eventful life of Minamoto-no-Yoshitsune was often taken up as a very popular theme of *Kabuki* and *jōruri* in the Edo period. Typical works include *"Kanjinchō"* (kabuki) and *"Yoshitsuné Senbonzakura"* (jōruri). In these works, it is not the most powerful figure (Yoritomo), but the tragic hero (Yoshitsuné), that wins more admiration.

Yoshitsuné's boyhood

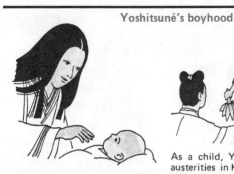

Tengu

Yoshitsuné was the child of Yoshitomo, commander-in-chief of the *Genji* family, had had with a court-lady. Though not so high in social standing, this lady is said to have been an exceptional beauty comparable to Ono-no-Komachi of Japan or Yang-kuei-fei of China.

As a child, Yoshitsuné practiced austerities in Kurama Temple with a view to becoming a *yamabushi* (esoteric Buddhist priest). Legend has it that he trained himself in martial arts with *tengu* (imaginary goblin looking like a human being with red face, long nose, and wings and having magic power) in the mountains of Kurama.

There was a very stout priest called Benkei. Believing that he was the strongest man in the world, Benkei was challenging *samurai* (warriors) living in Kyōto to a fight in succession, taking their swords from them. One day, he came across a handsome boy playing the flute. Benkei, in his usual way, challenged him to a fight with a view to getting his sword, only to be beaten by the young man who used nothing but his flute in the fight. This boy was Yoshitsuné. After that event, Benkei became a loyal follower of Yoshitsuné and shared his fate with his master.

The days of battle

Yoritomo

Yoshitsuné

Yoshitsuné visited Yoritomo when the latter raised an army of soldiers to overthrow the *Heishi* family. Having met together after an interval of more than ten years, they hugged each other and wept, pledging themselves to avenge the murder of their father Yoshitomo.

In the battle of Ichinotani (in Hyōgo Prefecture), the army of Yoshitsuné won a victory by making a surprise attack on the *Heishi* camp from the rear. It must have certainly been surprising to the *Heishi* army to realize that its enemy—men and horses—ran down a steep slope behind the camp, which slope could apparently be accessed only by wild deer.

It was Minamoto-no-Yoshinaka, cousin to Yoritomo, who was the first to enter the capital of Kyōto. Turning against Yoritomo, he attempted to become the ruler of the country. Perceiving Yoshinaka's ambition, Yoshitsuné drove the force of Yoshinaka away from Kyōto.

The *Heishi* family perished in the battle of Dannoura (the Shimonoseki Channel between Honshū and Kyūshū). In this battle, too, Yoshitsuné played the most active part, slashing about the enemy while jumping from one boat to another. Ironically, these brilliant achievements of Yoshitsuné in the series of battles with the *Heishi* family eventually led him to illfortune.

The days of elopement

Yoritomo, commander-in-chief of the *Genji* family, came to regard Yoshitsuné as his antagonist, and dispatched a large army to subjugate him. Defeated in a battle with Yoritomo's army, Yoshitsuné disguised himself as a *yamabushi* and wandered about the country, together with his lover Shizukagozen and loyal follower Benkei.

On the way, Shizukagozen had to part from Yoshitsuné at the foot of a mountain of no admittance to women. Eventually, she was captured by the army of Yoritomo. Though it is said that Shizukagozen was formerly a dancer, she has not been clearly identified.

Yoshitsuné visited a member of the Fujiwara family in the northeastern part of Honshu counting on their help. However, his lodging was raided by an army of Yoritomo who had received secret information from the Fujiwara family. In a shower of arrows all over his body, Benkei died standing firmly in front of the gate to Yoshitsuné's shelter. Standing at bay, Yoshitsuné killed himself.

In later ages, people thought that Yoshitsuné had actually escaped death and crossed the sea to China. Since the time at which they believed Yoshitsuné had fled to China coincided with the time at which Genhis Khan made his appearance in China, it was widely rumored that Yoshitsuné under the name of Genhis Khan had conquered East Asia.

HŌJŌ MASAKO
北条政子・1157—1225

Wife of Minamoto-no-Yoritomo, and mother of Minamoto-no-Yoriie and Minamoto-no-Sanetomo, both of whom became *shōgun*. When Sanetomo, the third *shōgun* of the Minamoto line, was assassinated in 1219, Hōjō Masako called a nominal *shōgun* in Kyōto to her at Kamakura, and installed her younger brother Hōjō Yoshitoki as *shikken** (important post to assist *shogun*), and thereby gained the helm of the Kamakura Shogunate. Because of her political ability and sharp temper uncommon with ordinary women, Masako was called a defacto woman *shōgun*.

After the death of Minamoto-no-Yoshitsuné, his lover Shizukagozen was called before Yoritomo to perform a dance. As she danced chanting to the loving memory of Yoshitsuné, Yoritomo went mad, almost killing her. But Masako dissuaded him from slaying Shizukagozen by saying that it was only natural for a woman to remember her beloved man.

After the death of Minamoto-no-Yoritomo, the base of the Kamakura Shogunate shock violently due to internal struggles for political supremacy. Yoriie, the second *shōgun,* was assassinated by Hōjō Tokimasa, father of Masako. Sanetomo, the third *shogun,* was also killed by a son of his elder brother Yoriie. Thus the Minamoto line ceased to exist. Thereafter, the reins of the Kamakura Shogunate passed to the *Hōjō* family.

The rebellion of ex-Emperor Gotoba

After Sanetomo was assassinated, the ex-Emperor Gotoba raised troops in Kyōto with a view to overthrowing the Kamakura Shogunate. Since war lords of the *Genji* family were entertaining antipathy against the Kamakura Shōgunate which had been under the control of the *Hōjō* family, the coup d'etat seemed to succeed. Facing the emergency, Masako consolidated the troops of the Shogunate by crying "Kill me before you take part with Gotoba!" in a large address before them.

Tomb of the Emperor Gotoba in Kyōto

Marching into Kyōto, the Shogunate troops were halted by the rushing current of the Uji River, when a fierce warrior named Sasaki Nobutsuna jumped into the current on his horse and crossed the river successfully. Encouraged by his feat, the Shogunate troops marched on to defeat the army of Gotoba. This battle is called *Jōkyū-no-Ran*.

Defeated in the battle, ex-Emperor Gotoba was exiled to Okinoshima island off the coast of Shimané Prefecture. There he died forlorn yearning for the days of lavish life in Kyōto. Toward the end of his life, he expressed his sentiment in the following poem:

"I am a new master of this island.
You, the raging wind,
Please calm down so my heart
won't be wounded."

UNKEI
運慶・1148—1223

Sculptors of statues of Buddha flourished in the early Kamakura period. Unkei renounced *"ichiboku-zukuri"* (method in which a statue of Buddha is carved from a solid wood block). Instead, he developed and completed a new technique called *"yosegi-zukuri"* (method in which a statue of Buddha is made by assembling the individual parts which are prefabricated). His style characterized by manliness and graveness was preferred by *samurai*. Many of his masterpieces remain intact.

Statue of Kongō-rikishi at Nandaimon Gate to Tōdai-ji Temple at Nara.

A feudal lord of a certain district called on Unkei living in Kyōto and asked him to work out a statue of Buddha, which he had completed. The Emperor happened to see the work and told Unkei that he must not allow such a masterpiece to be carried out of Kyōto. As this legend suggests, the works of Unkei were far superior to those of his contemporaries.

Statue of Miroku of Kōfuku-ji Temple at Nara

Priest of the late Heian period; founder of the *Jōdo-shū* sect. Hōnen entered the priesthood when he was fourteen years of age. Dissatisfied with existing Buddhism, he went his own way. Spiritually awakened at the age of 42, he preached that anyone could enter *Jōdo* (the Buddhist Elysian fields) after his death by reciting the prayer *"namu-amida-butsu."*

Hōnen stressed three things: true heart, piety, and wish to be reincarnated in *Jōdo*.

When Hōnen was eight years of age, his father was killed in a struggle for land ownership. On his deathbed, Hōnen's father said to him, "If you avenge me, the son of the opponent you slay will seek your life to avenge his father. Rather than continue such an endless fight of hatred, become a priest and perform a memorial service for me." It is said that Hōnen made up his mind to become a priest when he heard the last words of his father.

The teachings of Hōnen were enthusiastically accepted by the general mass because anyone, whether he be a noble or a peasant, was said to be spiritually saved by chanting a specific prayer. Because of this popularity, Hōnen was bitterly persecuted by existing Buddhist powers. At one time, he was condemned to exile, together with his followers.

SHINRAN
親鸞 · 1173—1262

Priest of the early Kamakura period; founder of the *Jōdoshin-shū* sect. Coming of a low-ranking noble family, Shinran enter-ed the priesthood at the age of nine. At 29, he became a dis-ciple of Hōnen, exercising a Buddhist invocation chanting '*Namu-amida-butsu*,' a prayer to Buddha. The *Jōdoshin-shū* sect founded by Shinran, and the *Nichiren-shū* sect which was also founded in the Kamakura period, have become the two leading sects of Japan's Buddhist world.

Nishi-hongan-ji Temple

Temples of the *Jōdoshin-shū* sect were called *Hongan-ji*, and the head temple was placed at Kyōto. As this Buddhist sect became ex-tremely powerful, the Tokugawa Shogunate (see p.92) divided the head temple into two: one in the east and one in the west.

Shinran teaches that anyone can enter *Jōdo* (Buddhist Elysian fields) only if he (or she) believes in *Amidabutsu*, the Buddha who saves every-body. His teachings are expressed by a simple term *"Tariki-Hongan."* He declared that meat-eating and matrimony were not contrary to the teachings of the Buddha. (Existing Buddhist sects denied those acts.) Therefore, the *Jōdoshin-shū* sect rapidly spread among many of those who wished to live a peaceful life after death, while seeking worldly benefits.

52

Ten years
十年

Ben'en

When he was nineteen years of age, Shinran had a revelation of Shōtoku Taishi (see p.14) in a dream, who told Shinran that he would not be able to live for more than 10 years. Hearing this dreamy prediction, Shinran devoted himself to learning with a view to freeing himself from the fear of death. He soon found, however, that none of the existing sects of Buddhism dispelled his fear. Ten years later, when he reached the age of 29, Shinran happened to meet Honen, who was to have a decisive influence on Shinran.

After the death of Hōnen, Shinran continued spreading the religion in Hitachi (Ibaragi Prefecture) while engaging himself in farming. Legend has it that one day Shinran was called on by a *yamabushi* named Ben'en, who had intended killing Shinran because he was envious of Shinran's fame, but that Ben'en was deeply impressed by the teachings of Shinran and eventually became his discipe.

Ikkō-Ikki

The teachings of Shinran received tremendous support of the general public, and in the Sengoku era* the believers under arms often staged a large-scale revolt against their feudal lord. Since they believed that they could live a peaceful life after their death, they never feared death in the fiercest battle. Because of this, even the powerful military commanders had considerable difficulty in putting down the revolts. The series of revolts was called *"ikkō-ikki,"* since the *Jōdoshin-shū* sect was also called the *Ikkō-shū* sect.

53

NICHIREN
日蓮・1222-1282

Priest of the Kamakura period; founder of the *Nichiren-shū* sect, one of Japan's leading sects of Buddhism. Nichiren entered the priesthood when he was twelve years of age. At 32, he reached the conclusion that the *Hokkekyō* was the one and only sacred book of Buddhism. As a result, he bitterly criticized all the other sects. Because of this, the life of Nichiren was characterized by a successor of fights against religious persecution.

During a journey, Nichiren died of sickness at Ikegami Hongan-ji Temple at the age of 61. Even today, a meeting in memory of Nichiren is held at Ikegami Hongan-ji Temple (in Tōkyō) on October 12 and 13 every year.

Nichiren taught that anyone could achieve oneness with the Buddha by reciting the *'Nammyō-hōren-gekyō'* representing the truth of the *Hokkekyō*. Since he preached that only his sect could save the country, he was condemned to exile by the *Shōgun* angered to hear that.

Spiritually awakened, Nichiren traveled around the country spreading his teachings. As he maintained that believers in any sect other than his would go to hell, he was often abused in foul language and even pelted with pebbles occasionally.

Having excited the Shogunate's anger by his radical doctrine, Nichiren was sentenced to death. Legend has it that when the executioner was about to behead Nichiren, thunder rolled suddenly and a thunderbolt broke the sword.

Nichiren thus escaped execution, but was condemned to exile to the Island of Sado. There he was confined in a small house which had been used to accommodate dead prisoners. Nevertheless, he kept his belief and continued spreading the religion on the island.

Nichiren had predicted that unless the Shogunate believed in the *Nichiren-shū* sect, the country would suffer from a foreign invasion. Soon after his prediction, attempts to invade Japan were made by the Mongols. As Nichiren's prediction came true, people respecting him increased in number rapidly. This helped the remarkable spread of the *Nichiren-shū* sect.

Military commander of the Nambokuchō period; known as strategic genius. Supporting Emperor Godaigo who was aiming to overthrow the Kamakura Shogunate, Kusunoki Masashigé led a small army to defeat a large army of the Shogunate in a series of battles. However, as the Emperor administered the affairs of state in favor of the court nobles, discontent among the military class mounted. Masashigé sided with the Emperor to the very last and died a violent death. Along with Minamoto-no-Yoshitsuné and Sanada-Yukimura, Masashigé is one of the most popular military commanders who died a heroic death.

**Strategic Feats
of Kusunoki-Masashigé**

A strong force of the Kamakura Shogunate advanced to Akasaka Castle (in Ōsaka) in which Kusunoki Masashigé and his force had entrenched temselves. It was apparently a small castle built in the middle of an open field. The shogunate army thought that they would be able to capture such a castle in one day.

Thousands of shogunate soldiers crossed a bridge over the moat and reached the outer wall of the castle, when the bridge suddenly collapsed, isolating them from the main force of the shogunate.

When the invaders who could no longer retreat tried to climb the outer wall, the wall crumbled, pushing them down into a deep ditch. From behind the fallen wall appeared the original wall.

Astounded by Masashige's cunning plan, the shogunate army abandoned the plan to attack the enemy directly. Instead, the commander-in-chief decided to besiege the castle and cut off the food supply. Since the shogunate force was then ten times the force of Masashige, there was no chance to Masashige winning a protracted battle.

So, Masashigé stacked bodies of enemy soldiers on the ground and set them on fire. Looking at the fire, the shogunate army thought that Masashigé had committed suicide, and marched into the castle. There they found that Masashigé's army had sneaked out during the night.

ASHIKAGA TAKAUJI
足利尊氏・1305—1358

First *Shōgun* of the Muromachi Shogunate. One of the military commanders serving the Kamakura Shogunate. Ashikaga Takauji joined the scheme of Emperor Godaigo to overthrow the Shogunage. He played a leading part in enabling the Emperor to restore imperial authority. Eventually, however, Takauji organized a rebel army of *samurai* warriors who were frustrated by the aristocracy of Godaigo. After he expelled the Emperor Godaigo from Kyōto, Takauji set up a military government — the Muromachi Shogunate.

Tenryū-ji Temple

When Emperor Godaigo of the hostile South court died, Takauji built Tenryū-ji Temple at Kyōto to the memory of the Emperor.

Until the end of World War II, Ashikaga Takauji had been branded as a traitor to Japan's imperial dynasty and his name had been intentionally omitted from history textbooks. According to traditional belief, however, Takauji was placid and generous, hence very popular among *samurai* warriors.

Emperor Godaigo

Ashikaga Takauji was a military commander who had excellent judgment on the state of things. When he was ordered from the Kamakura Shogunate to subjugate the Emperor Godaigo, he was well aware of the fact that *samurai* warriors had already been estranged from the *Hōjō* family. On his way to Kyōto, Takauji sent a letter to the Emperor recommending that the shogunate be overthrown then.

Commended by the Emperor Godaigo as he most valiant player in the overthrow of the Kamakura shogunate, Takauji was endowed with three provinces. By that time, however, he had already noticed that *samurai* warriors were highly discontented with the aristocracy of Godaigo. With this recognition, Takauji eventually made up his mind to organize his army so as to overthrow the imperial court and set up a new military government.

Tomb of Takauji
in Kyōto

Counterattacked by the troops of Kusunoki Masashigé and some other military commanders, Takauji once retreated to Kyūshū, but soom organized a big army of hundreds of thousands of soldiers and marched into Kyōto. Having expelled Emperor Godaigo, he backed Emperor Kōmyō to grip real political power in his hands.

Despite glories of his best days, Takauji was far from happy in his last years. Exhausted by power struggles among his children and the battles with the South imperial court, he came to believe in Buddhism and practiced the austerity of the *Zen* sect. Eventually, he contracted a malignant skin disease and died in agony.

ASHIKAGA YOSHIMITSU
足利義満・1358—1408

Third *Shōgun* of the Muromachi Shogunate. Ashikaga Yoshimitsu put an end to the confrontation between the South and North imperial courts and subjugated powerful clans in various parts of the country, thereby securing shogunate control of the whole nation. He made huge profits from trade with the Ming dynasty of China. Yoshimitsu preferred pompous culture and art. The famous Kinkaku-ji Temple at Kyōto was built by him.

Kinkaku-ji Temple

The original Kinkaku-ji Temple was a three-tier building constructed on the ground of Rokuon-ji Temple at Kyōto. The walls, ceilings, and even pillars, had gold coating. This structure was destroyed by fire in 1950. The Kinkaku-ji Temple as seen today was built in 1955.

Muromachi period
Son of the Second *Shōgun* Yoshiakira, Yoshimitsu ascended the shogunate when he was only 10. At the age of 20, he built a magnificent residence at Muromachi in Kyōto and made sure that the spacious garden was kept full of a variety of flowering plants all year round. People called this residence *'hana-no-gosho'* (Imperial palace of flowers). The name 'Muromachi Shogunate' originates in this residence at Muromachi.

Eighth *Shōgun* of the Muromachi Shogunate. The reign of Ashikaga-Yoshimasa was characterized by violent political power struggles of the shogunate, as peasants were uniting themselves more strongly than ever and raising *'ikki'* (peasants' mobbing) frequently in various parts of the country. In his last years, Yoshimasa lost interest in politics completely, causing the struggle among possible successors to become fiercer. Eventually, the Battle of *Ōnin,* which was to reduce Kyōto to ruins, broke out, marking the start of the Sengoku period — the age of rivalry of local war lords.

← Ginkaku-ji Temple

Ginkaku-ji Temple is a temple dedicated to *Kannon* (Goddess of Mercy) which was built by Yoshimasa at Higashiyama after Kinkaku-ji Temple built by Yoshimitsu at Kitayama. In contrast to pompous Kinkaku-ji Temple, Ginkaku-ji Temple has a mellow air, reflecting the desolate social conditions of those days.

Battle of Ōnin

Civil war which took place in and around Kyōto for 11 years from 1467 to 1477. The war was really a power struggle between two leading military commanders of the Muromachi Shogunate. As both armies — total number of soldiers some 250,000 — fought a violent fight in the capital Kyōto, the shogunate lost its authority. In the meantime, Yoshimasa confined himself in his villa (Ginkaku-ji Temple), showing no interest in what was happening just outside his temporary residence.

ZEAMI
世阿弥・1363—1443

Noh actor of the Muromachi period. Under the patronage of the third *shōgun* Ashikaga-Yoshimitsu, Zeami, together with his father Kan,ami, produced excellent *Noh* dramas featuring both dignity and popularity. His treatise on *Noh* titled *"Fūshi-kaden"* has long been a bible for *Noh* players. This book is also helpful in understanding the Japanese sense of beauty.

Kobeshimi
(male demon)

Ko-omote
(young woman)

In *Noh* drama, the leading player is called *shité* and the by-player, *waki*. *Noh* dance is highly abstract and may be regarded as an ultimate form of Japanese art of public entertainment. On the other hand, the *Noh* drama in its present form is too difficult to be fully appreciated even by Japanese spectators without the aid of the text.

Originally, the term *"Noh"* referred to performances in music and dancing of itinerant players. Then it came to refer to *sarugaku* (literally, monkey music), which swiftly became very popular in the early Muromachi period. *Sarugaku* is a form of entertainment featuring humorous mimicry. The noble class despised *sarugaku* as a base accomplishment. It was two celebrated playwrights and actors, father and son, Kan'ami and Zeami, that refined the 'base' accomplishment to a respectable art.

When Zeami was twelve years of age, he, together with his father Kan'ami, played a *Noh* drama before the *Shōgun* Yoshimitsu. Deeply impressed by Kan'ami's superb performance and Zeami's rare beauty, Yoshimitsu decided to give them his hearty patronage.

Zeami was in his prime when at the age of 40 he played *Noh* before the Emperor and the *shōgun.* He was highly successful in his efforts to sublimate *Noh,* an art of public entertainment, to a unique aesthetics called *yūgen* (subtlety) without impairing its liveliness.

However, the fourth *Shōgun* Ashikaga Yoshimochi who succeeded Yoshimitsu on his death disliked Zeami and forbade him from appearing on stage. Zeami in despair devoted himself to writing *Fūshikaden* with a view to transmitting the essence of *Noh* to future generations.

Toward the end of his life, Zeami was still more unfortunate. He lost two of his sons he had hoped to become his successors, and he himself was exiled to the Island of Sado. Details about the last few years of Zeami are unknown.

Zen priest of the Muromachi period. Ikkyū Sōjun was born of a common family in Kyōto, though the unfounded rumor that he was an illegitimate offspring of the emperor spread later. When he was six years of age, he entered a temple of *Zen* Buddhism. At 16, he criticized the existing *Zen* sect as corrupt. After assiduously practicing austerity, he was spiritually awakened at 27. Thereafter, he endeavored to spread the teachings of the *Zen* sect among the general masses.

Ikkyū's hermitage in the Daitoku-ji Temple at Kyōto had no *shōji* (paper-fitted sliding screens), allowing rain and snow to enter the room directly. This unique setup represents his idea that one's spirit could be trained not only by appreciating beautiful nature but also by standing harsh nature.

Ikkyū seldom stayed at a particular temple for long. He spent most of his time making pilgrimages to various parts of the country. According to tradition, he intentionally sought humble temples for his lodgings because he disliked big temples, which he thought were bent on making money. He displayed exceptional wisdom and sense of humor from his childhood. As amusing anecdota told of him were compiled into a book of great popularity in the Edo period, Ikkyū became very popular among the general public.

As a child, Ikkyū was called before the *Shōgun* Ashikaga Yoshimitsu, who jokingly ordered him to rope up a tiger in a picture drawn on one of the panels of a folding screen. To this, Ikkyū smiled and said that he would tie up the tiger as soon as the *shōgun* drove it out of the picture.

Wooden sword

At times, Ikkyū carried about with him a wooden sword. Asked about the reason, Ikkyū answered, "This sword is a sham one, hence cannot be a murderous weapon. Present-day Buddhism is a deception, hence cannot save mankind."

A celebrated *Zen* priest, Ikkyū was also noted for his peculiar behavior. On every New Year's Day, Ikkyū carried about with him a stick with a skull atop, saying, "True, the New Year's Day is a day to be celebrated. But, each time one greets the New Year, he takes a step toward his death*. Hence, New Year's Day is really a day on which one should earnestly meditate on his way of life for the year."

* Formerly in Japan, one's age was incremented by 1 on each New Year's Day regardless of one's actual birthday.

SESSHŪ
雪舟・1420—1506

Painter and *Zen* priest of the Muromachi period. In his childhood, Sesshū began to practice *Zen* austerity and learn *suibokuga* (black-and-white painting). At the age of 48, he crossed the sea to Ming China. After he returned home, he created many superb black-and-white paintings, mainly *sansui-ga* (landscape paintings), the theme of which was natural landscape.

Sesshū was also a prominent *Zen* priest. It is said that he came at the top of the class soon after he entered a famous temple of *Zen* Buddhism in China.

Part of *"Sansui-chōkan,"* one of Sesshu's masterpieces

In the days when Sesshū just began practicing austerity, he was bent on drawing pictures. One day, his teacher bound Sesshū to a column of the Buddhist sanctum with a view to stopping his indulgence.

After it grew dark, the teacher came to Sesshū thinking it was about time to set him free, when a mouse jumped from near Sesshū's tiptoe. To his surprise, it was really a picture of a mouse drawn by Sesshū in his teardrops using his big toe.

Sesshū presented the Ming Dynasty with his painting of a Japanese temple called Seiken-ji. After he returned home, he found that the five-storied pagoda he had drawn did not exist. Ashamed to let his painting be inaccurate, he contributed a five-storied pagoda to the Seiken-ji Temple.

In the garden of Tōfuku-ji Temple at Kyōto, there are a stone crane and a stone tortoise which are said to be the work of Sesshū. When he heard that the stone tortoise had moved about the garden at night, the legend goes, he drove a long piece of stone into the tortoise's back to nail it down. As a result, the figure of the stone tortoise became what it is today.

HŌJŌ SŌUN
北条早雲・1432—1519

As political control of the Muromachi Shogunate waned, a new type of local landlord called *sengoku daimyō* emerged in various parts of the country. *Sengoku daimyō* possessed their own army and political system, and were administering their own domain independently of the shogunate, each aiming at unifying the country individually. This was the beginning of the Sengoku period, the most dramatic era in Japanese history. Hojo Soun was one of those *sengoku daimyō* of the early Sengoku period

Notice board

Hōjō Sōun thought that political stability could be secured only when the ruler won the confidence of farmers in his domain. According to tradition, he looked after the interests of the farmers by cutting the rate of land tax (paid in rice) to 40%, so that when he got involved in a battle, his farmers fought for him at the risk of their lives.

Hōjō Sōun was a low-level *samurai* warrior. However, when he became a vassal of *shugo daimyō* (local landlord appointed by the shogunate) of the Province of Suruga (Shizuoka), he began to distinguish himself. He subjugated the feudal lord of Izu in Shizuoka (when he was 60) and the feudal lord of Kanagawa (when he was 85), thereby gaining control of their domains.

MŌRI MOTONARI
毛利元就・1497—1571

Notable military commander of the Sengoku period. Born as second son of a minor feudal lord, Mōri Motonari went on to become a ruler of the entire Chūgoku district by his resourcefulness. His teaching of three arrows is well known among the Japanese. Incidentally, it was quoted in the introduction to the motion picture *"Ran"* directed by Akira Kurosawa.

One day, Motonari handed an arrow to each of his three sons, and ordered them to break their arrows. Each of them could break his arrow easily. Then, Motonari ordered each to break three arrows bound together. None of the three sons could break the bundle of arrows. By this, Motonari tought his sons that they would not be able to beat a powerful enemy if they fought separately, but that they surely could if they united themselves against one.

When he was twelve years of age, Mōri Motonari, followed by a vassal, visited the shrine. On their way home, Motonari asked the vassal what he had prayed for. The vassal answered, "I prayed my Lord would be able to become the ruler of the Province of Aki (Hiroshima)." On hearing this, Motonari regretfully said, "There is a saying that 'Ask for an ell, and you get an inch.' If so, you should have prayed that our Lord would be able to become the ruler of the whole country."

TAKEDA SHINGEN
武田信玄・1521—1573

Sengoku daimyō of the Province of Kai (Yamanashi Prefecture). Celebrated statesman and military commander, Takeda Shingen was exalted as the strongest warrior of the Sengoku period. A series of battles he fought against Uesugi Kenshin, Oda Nobunaga, Tokugawa Ieyasu, and other powerful *daimyō* have been taken up in many novels and motion pictures as the most dramatic events of the Sengoku period.

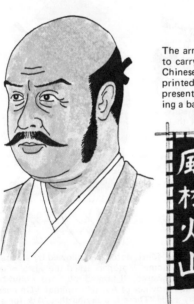

The army of Takeda Shingen used to carry a standard on which four Chinese characters 風林火山 were printed. These characters aptly represented Shingen's way of fighting a battle. Thus,

(hū)
— Be as swift as wind

(rin)
— Be as silent as the wood

(ka)
— Attack as fierily as fire

(zan)
— Be as composed as the mountain

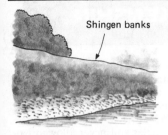

Shingen banks

Takeda Shingen was also a notable administrator. He did much to protect the living of people within his domain. In order to prevent the flooding of rivers, he spent huge amounts of money to construct banks along the rivers.
These banks called *Shingen-zutsumi* still remain in Yamanashi Prefecture.

Shingen's famous expression is "Man is a castle, a stone wall, and a moat: sympathy is a friend; hatred is an enemy." These words concisely represent his belief that building a strong army was winning the confidence of the people.

Shingen's daughter   Oda Nobunaga's son

Shingen intended to expand his influence not only by force but also by expedient marriage. To this end, he took a number of wives and married his daughters to sons of *daimyō* of the neighboring provinces. To the *daimyō* of the Sengoku period, daughters were often a tool to conciliate their rivals.

When Shingen was fifty years of age, he led a large army toward Kyōto aiming at unifying the whole country. He defeated the allied forces of Oda Nobunaga and Tokugawa Ieyasu, but died of sickness just before he could attain his goal. According to traditional belief, Uesugi Kenshin, on hearing the death of Shingen, said in tears that he had lost a worthy opponent.

UESUGI KENSHIN
上杉謙信・1530—1578

Celebrated military commander of the Sengoku period. Ruler of the Province of Echigo (Niigata Prefecture), Uesugi Kenshin was the most formidable rival to Takeda Shingen who was governing the neighboring Province of Kai (Yamanashi Prefecture). According to traditional belief, he was a guileless, brave general who adhered to his principles and never allowed women to come near all his life.

Salt

A certain military commander who was antagonistic to Takeda Shingen stopped the shipment of salt to the Province of Kai. Since salt could not be produced in the landlocked province, the people living in Shingen's domain suffered much from the salt embargo. When Uesugi Kenshin heard that fact, he immediately had ample amounts of salt sent to his rival Takeda Shingen saying that *samurai* must play fair and should not resort to dirty tricks at any time.

Like other contemporary military commanders, Uesugi Kenshin was dreaming of going to the capital of Kyōto and gaining sway over the whole country. His ambition was largely frustrated by his defeat in a fierce battle with Takeda Shingen at Kawanakajima on the provincial border and by the stout resistance of believers in the *Jōdoshin-shū* sect which had taken root in Echigo since propagation by Shinran. At last, in 1578, Kenshin led large army toward Kyōto, but died of illness along the way.

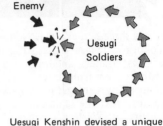

The army of Uesugi Kenshin carried a standard bearing the Chinese character 毘 . This character was taken from 毘沙門天 (pronounced *'bishamonten'*), the God of warriors.

Uesugi Kenshin devised a unique offensive disposition in which soldiers forming a circle advanced while turning. This proved extremely effective, since when a soldier fell down the next one was ready to fight.

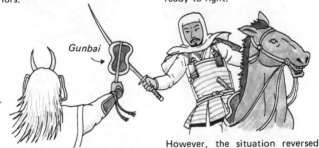

Gunbai

Uesugi Kenshin and Takeda Shingen fought each other five times in the Battle of Kawanakajima. In the fight of 1561, the troops of Kenshin attacked Shingen's headquarters at night, outmaneuvering Shingen who had divided his troops into two with a view to attacking the enemy from both sides.

However, the situation reversed when a detached force of Shingen attacked Kenshin's troops in the rear. Kenshin then rushed alone on horseback into Shingen's main camp and struck at Shingen with his sword. Shingen caught the blow with his iron fan. At the same time, one of his vassals thrust Kenshin's horse buttock with his sword, saving Shingen who was almost killed.

ODA NOBUNAGA
織田信長・1534—1582

It was three heroes — Oda Nobunaga, Toyotomi Hideyoshi, and Tokugawa Ieyasu — that struggled through the Sengoku period of rival leaders and reunified the country. A highly-gifted military commander, Oda Nobunaga aimed at unifying the country by subjugating *sengoku daimyō* of various provinces by force. At the same time, he positively introduced advanced cultures of Western countries, thereby bringing a new social order out of chaos. Thus, it may be said that he was one of the Japan's greatest revolutionists.

Nobunaga's character was aptly described by a famous *haiku* (17-syllable poem):
"Na-ka-nu-na-ra   Ko-ro-shi-te-shi-ma-é Ho-to-to-gi-gu"
(The cuckoo doesn't sing? All right, kill it at once.)
At this *haiku* suggests, Nobunaga liquidated all his antagonists on his way to national unification.

Oda Nobunaga was born as a son of a minor landlord of the Province of Owari(Aichi Pref.), which was surrounded by domains under control of powerful daimyō. Since Nobunaga's domain was a rich country where agriculture and commerce were flourishing, it was constantly sought after by his rival daimyō and even his brothers and relatives. In such a critical neighborhood, Nobunaga's unusual faith in power was taking shape.

Nobunaga in His Youth

Sack full of food, stones, and junks

Saitō Dōsan

Nobunaga in his teens was an untidily-dressed, ill-mannered, and impudent fellow. So people gossiped that the young lord of Oda was a downright fool.

One day Nobunaga, untidily dressed as usual, came to the front gate of the residence of Saitō Dōsan, a powerful *daimyō*, with a view to meeting him. When Nobunaga appeared before Dōsan, however, he had changed into formal *samurai* attire without being noticed by anyone. Dōsan then thought with admiration that Nobunaga must be attired slovenly with the intention to deceive others. Later, Dōsan noted that when he died his domain would be captured by that man.

According to legend, Nobunaga attended his father's funeral with his sword held between his side and a straw rope wound around his waist, and threw a handful of incense powder at the father's body before the company.

The *samurai* who had served as a guardian for Nobunaga held himself responsible for Nobunaga's eccentric behavior and committed *hara-kiri*. It is said that the suicide of his guardian led Nobunaga to devote himself to martial arts.

The Battle of Okehazama

Nobunaga had an army only 2,000 strong when Imagawa Yoshimoto, a powerful *daimyō*, led a 25,000-men army into Nobunaga's domain. If Nobunaga were a mediocre military commander, he would have yielded to the invaders at once. Actually, he behaved himself differently. While the enemy was approaching, Nobunaga performed a dance in his castle saying in singsong fashion, "Man can live for only 50 years at longest. Every man is destined to die sooner or later."

After the performance, Nobunaga followed by his 2,000 soldiers made a surprise attack on Imagawa's main camp in a heavy rain. Imagawa's forces which had been elated with their previous victories were put to rout. In this battle, commander-in-chief Imagawa Yoshimoto fell in action. Thus Nobunaga's 2,000-men army defeated the much bigger army of Imagawa. As a result, Nobunaga increased his influence dramatically.

The Battle of Nagashino

In the Battle of Nagashino, Nobunaga's army was confronted by the army of horsemen, which was commonly acknowledged as the strongest army of the Sengoku period, led by Takeda Katsuyori. This time, Nobunaga had a stockade and ditch built to check the advance of the enemy horses, and disposed a firearm troop in three rows in the ditch, from where they fired at the enemy forces checked by the stockade. This was the first battle fight in Japan in which guns were used systematically.

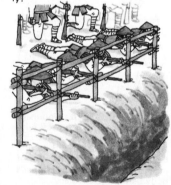

On the Road to National Unification

In the Sengoku period, an armed group of believers in the *Ikkō-shū** sect of Buddhism emerged as a new army, which was as strong as that of a feudal lord. In subjugating the army of adherents of the *Ikkō-shū* sect, Nobunaga put up a fence around the fortress in which some 20,000 men and women were entrenching themselves so as to prevent them from escaping, and then set fire to the fortress from all sides, burning all of them to death.

Oda Nobunaga protected Christianity, as well as promoting trade with the Portuguese and the Dutch. As a result, there was a flow of western art, scholarship, tools and other foreign culture into Japan.

After gaining control of the eastern half of Japan, Nobunaga led his army westwards with a view to unifying the whole country. Along the way, Akechi Mitsuhidé, one of Nobunaga's subordinate military commanders, followed by his 10,000-men army, attacked Nobunaga at Honnō-ji Temple where he had taken up his lodgings. At that moment, there were only about 70 guards in and around the temple. Becoming aware of the treachery of his subordinate, Nobunaga killed himself in the temple bursting into flames.

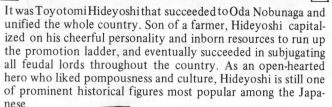

TOYOTOMI HIDEYOSHI
豊臣秀吉・1536—1598

It was Toyotomi Hideyoshi that succeeded to Oda Nobunaga and unified the whole country. Son of a farmer, Hideyoshi capitalized on his cheerful personality and inborn resources to run up the promotion ladder, and eventually succeeded in subjugating all feudal lords throughout the country. As an open-hearted hero who liked pompousness and culture, Hideyoshi is still one of prominent historical figures most popular among the Japanese.

Hideyoshi's character was aptly described by the following *haiku* poem:
"Na-ka-nu-na-ra Na-ka-sé-té-mi-sé-yō Ho-to-to-gi-su"
(The cuckoo doesn't sing? All right, I'll let it sing.)
As this *haiku* suggests, Hideyoshi always made his best to improve his lot for himself no matter how difficult a situation he was in.

Ōsaka Castle

The magnificent Ōsaka Castle at Ōsaka is symbolic of the one-time glory of Toyotomi Hideyoshi. This castle was built by some 60,000 laborers in two and a half years. Huge volumes of stone used for the castle were carried in on more than 1,000 vessels from various parts of the country. Today the castle is one of the most prominent symbols of Ōsaka.

Born as a son of a poor farmer in the Province of Owari (Aichi Prefecture), Hideyoshi was bereft of his father when he was very young. According to legend, he led a miserable life in his childhood, as he was ill-treated by his father-in-law. Such being the case, he left home at the age of 14 in search of a military career.

One of European missionaries who had met Hideyoshi described him as an ugly-looking man with popped eyes, lacking in dignity. When young, Hideyoshi as nicknamed "Monkey."

On one unusual cold winter morning, Hideyoshi, who had entered the service of Oda Nobunaga, was warming Nobunaga's *zōri* (Japanese sandals) in his bosom. When Nobunaga saw that, he rewarded Hideyoshi for his good mental attitude. Hideyoshi ascended the promotion ladder one rung after another by keeping on doing such commendable deeds.

Having become a military commander under Nobunaga, Hideyoshi distinguished himself in the battle against the Saito family of Mino Province (Gifu Prefecture). According to legend, Hideyoshi had newly-cut logs carried on rafts down the river into the enemy's territory, where he had a fortress built overnight to defeat the enemy.

Mōri's family

Toyotomi Hideyoshi

When Akechi Mitsuhidé attacked Nobunaga to death, Hideyoshi was fighting with the Mōri family of the Chūgoku district. On hearing the death of his master Nobunaga, Hideyoshi made peace with Mōri and led all his troops back to Kyōto in only 10 days. The reason why Hideyoshi could outdo other powerful feudal lords to succeed Nobunaga was ascribable partly to his quick action in avenging his master by punishing Mitsuhidé.

Defeated in the competition against Hideyoshi, Akechi Mitsuhidé fled Kyōto. On his way of escape, Mitsuhidé was attacked by a gang of farmers and stabbed with a bamboo-spear to death. Since Mitsuhidé was in power for a very short peroid, his reign was called *"Mitsuhidé's mikka-tenka"* (literally, three-day reign).

'Kenchi' and 'Katana-gari'

After unifying the whole country, Hideyoshi established a nation-wide land surveying system called *"kenchi"* with a view to keeping an accurate record of financial power of each of local feudal lords.

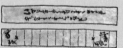

measure used in Kenchi

Also, Hideyoshi enforced a law called *"Katana-gari,"* which strictly prohibited any person other than *samurai* from keeping a sword or any other type of weapon. In the Sengoku period, a large-scale riot (*"ikki"*) by a mass of armed farmers occurred frequently at various parts of the country. The purpose of *katana-gari* was to deprive non-*samurai* classes of arms, thereby preventing *ikki*.

Toward the end of his life, Hideyoshi was dreaming of conquering Korea, China, and India to become King of East Asia. As a preparation for his planned invasion into China, he studied the Chinese language holding a big folding fan with a map of Japan, China, and Korea drawn on one side and a Chinese vocabulary, pronunciations, and meanings written on the other.

Hideyoshi dispatched a big army of more than 150,000 soldiers to the Korean peninsula in 1587 and 1597, respectively. Although Hideyoshi's troops armed with guns could outdo the Korean army which had not any guns, they were eventually forced to retreat by steadfast resistance of the Korean masses. The unsuccessful expedition to Korea caused Hideyoshi's power of his last years to wane gradually.

Hideyoshi was a devotee of *sadō* (the way of tea). Among others, the big tea ceremony held in the forest of Kitano Shrine at Kyōto under the sponsorship of Hideyoshi was crowded with the thousands of participants, since all people — *samurai* and commoners — were allowed to participate and see Hideyoshi making ceremonial tea.

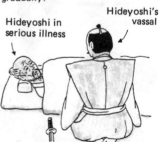

Hideyoshi in serious illness

Hideyoshi's vassal

When Hideyoshi died, his son and heir Hideyori was only six years of age. Full of anxiety about the future of Hideyori, Hideyoshi continued to ask his subordinate feudal lords to take good care of Hideyori, till his death.

SANADA YUKIMURA
真田幸村・1567—1615

Military commander of the Sengoku period. As the commander-in-chief of the Toyotomi army, Sanada Yukimura fought a brave fight against the Tokugawa army aiming at capturing the Ōsaka Castle. He enjoyed a high reputation as a distinguished commander as he trifled with the big army of Tokugawa by his wealth of resources. He has been treated as a hero in many novels and motion pictures. Thus, along with Kusunoki Masashigé, who was a resourceful general of the Nambokuchō period, Yukimura has become one of the foremost legendary commanders.

The standard marked with *"roku-ren-sen"* (six coins in two columns), symbol of the Sanada army

Sanada Masayuki

Sanada Yukimura

Sanada Nobuyuki

Sanada Yukimura had the second son of Sanada Masayuki who was a minor feudal lord of Shinshū (Nagano Prefecture). In the Battle of Sekigahara, Masayuki and Yukimura sided with Toyotomi, while Nobuyuki, the first son of Masayuki, joined Tokugawa. It is said that Masayuki let his two sons join the opposing parties so that the Sanada family could survive regardless of which party won the battle.

After Yukimura entered the Ōsaka Castle, he built a citadel named *"Sanada-maru"* on the front, from which his army confronted Tokugawa's 300,000-men army. He lured enemy troops into an empty moat and let his gunmen shoot at them, causing huge damage to the enemy.

Then, he led 3,500 soldiers into the main camp of Tokugawa. Under the violent attack of the troops led by Yukimura, the body-guards of Tokugawa Ieyasu were put to rout. Yukimura and his men closed in upon Ieyasu, when Tokugawa's main force of 100,000 soldiers arrived at the scene. At the end of a fierce battle, the Sanada army was totally destroyed and Yukimura died a violent death.

Although Sanada Yukimura had foreseen the defeat of the Toyotomi army, he fought against an overwhelmingly big army of Tokugawa and died a heroic death for his fidelity to the Toyotomi family. Since Yukimura was a man of the type favored by the majority of Japanese, he became a legendary hero after his death. In the Meiji era, in particular, fictions dealing with heroic deeds of Yukimura and his squad of *ninja* (masters of the art of invisibility) became very popular.

Kirigakuré Saizō
One of *Jū-yūshi* and notable *ninja*.

Sarutobi Sasuké
Protean Iga-style *ninja*. Most prominent of Yukimura's *"Jū-yūshi"* (ten brave vassals), he became the leading character in many of the popular fictions dealing with *ninja* in the Meiji era.

ISHIDA MITSUNARI
石田三成・1560—1600

Military commander of the Azuchi-Momoyama period. As a young boy, Ishida Mitsunari impressed Toyotomi Hideyoshi as a man of brilliant talent. When Hideyoshi came to power, Mitsunari was appointed to an important post in the government at the age of 25. He proved to be an excellent administrator under the reign of Hideyoshi. In the Battle of Sekigahara (1600), he led the Toyotomi army (west camp) against the Tokugawa army (east camp). Defeated in the competition, Mitsunari was beheaded.

Mitsunari on the cart to execution place

To the last moment of his death, Ishida Mitsunari remained loyal to his master Hideyoshi. When he was being beheaded, he glared right at his one-time comrades who had went over to Tokugawa. It is said that most of those betrayers sneaked away from the scene, with their eyes cast down.

After the death of Toyotomi Hideyoshi, his vassals split into two groups: one headed by Ishida Mitsunari who wished to rule the country by administrative means, and the other headed by Katō Kiyomasa who insisted upon suppressing antagonistic parties by military means. Taking advantage of their confrontation, Tokugawa Ieyasu increased his power rapidly. Undoubtedly, the internal discord was one of major factors contributing to fatal defeat of Toyotomi in the Battle of Sekigahara.

KATŌ KIYOMASA
加藤清正・1562—1611

Military commander of the Sengoku period. A vassal of Toyotomi Hideyoshi, Katō Kiyomasa was noted for his fearless courage. Since Kiyomasa was on bad terms with Ishida Mitsunari, he did not join the Battle of Sekigahara in which Mitsunari commanded the Toyotomi army. For that reason, Kiyomasa could secure a fief at Kumamoto in Kyūshū after Tokugawa Ieyasu came to power. He displayed his talent in civil engineering and had great confidence of his people. He was also known as a devotee of the *Nichiren-shū* sect of Buddhism.

Katō Kiyomasa was a master hand at wielding a spear. According to legend, in a certain battle, he rushed into the enemy's gunman troops while wielding a spear as long as 5 meters, and killed the commander. Another legend has it that during the Korean expedition, he speared a big tiger to death.

When Kiyomasa led his army back from Korea to Japan, he ordered the fully-equipped soldiers to march in battle formation through a plain where they did not see even the shadow of a single enemy as far as the eye could reach. As a military man, he knew well that a split second of incautiousness could lead him to death.

SEN-NO-RIKYŪ
千利休・1522—1591

Master of *"sadō"* of the Azuchi-Momoyama period. Tea-lover from his childhood, Sen-no-Rikyū taught *sadō* (the way of tea) to the two great military commanders, Oda Nobunaga and Toyotomi Hideyoshi. By introducing the *Zen* spirits of *"wabi"* (quiet elegance) and *"sabi"* (quaintness) into *sadō,* which had been not more than a taste among the *samurai* and noble classes, he refined *sadō* to the level of art.

Rikyū lies in the garden of Jukō-in Temple on the grounds of Dai-toku-ji Temple at Kyōto. It is said that the tombstone was modeled after the image of a sacred fire of Buddha.

Sadō refers to etiquette and formalities to be observed when making tea for a guest. The terms *"wabi"* and *"sabi"* represent a unique sense of Japanese who find real beauty in something common and plain, rather than apparent pompousness. *Rikyū* embodied this sense of beauty in everything from etiquette and formalities of *sadō* to the tearoom, tea garden, and every piece of tea utensil, thereby creating an aesthetic space which might be called a microcosm.

Rikyū had generous patronage of Toyotomi Hideyoshi. Whenever Hideyoshi, as the sovereign of the country, invited a noble or feudal lord from various parts of the country, he let Rikyū prepare tea for his guest. Hideyoshi also generously promoted Rikyū to a responsible post of his government. As many feudal lords became pupils of Rikyū, Rikyū came to wield enormous influence.

One day, Katō Kiyomasa, one of the foremost vassals of Hideyoshi, tought he should kill Rikyū to stop Hideyoshi getting involved too much in *sadō*. However, he was surprised to find that Rikyū was thoroughly on the alert while making tea. Deeply impressed by the exquisite atmosphere created by Rikyū, Kiyomasa completely forgot to slay Rikyū.

Main gate of Daitoku-ji Temple

When Rikyū had a wooden statue of himself set atop the main gate of Daitoku-ji Temple, Hideyoshi got mad and ordered Rikyū to commit *hara-kiri*. The reason was that he just could not allow a wooden statue of any of his vassals to be set upon a gate under which he was likely to pass.

Rikyū committed *hara-kiri* in a tearoom named Kan'inseki of Daitoku-ji Temple. After Rikyū died, his sons founded three schools of *sado, Omoté-senké, Ura-senké,* and *Mushanokōji-senké,* which have been in existence to date.

IZUMO-NO-OKUNI
出雲阿国 · 16–17th century

Actress of the late Azuchi-Momoyama period to the early Edo period; known as the originator of *Kabuki*. According to one legend, Izumo-no-Okuni was a virgin in service of Izumo Shrine, one of Japan's leading *shintō* shrines. Another legend has it that she was a professional dancer who traveled around the country for her living. In any case, her private life is shrouded in mystery. With the social unrest that followed the Battle of Sekigahara in the background, a decadent style of performance by a girls' operetta company led by Izumo-no-Okuni won sweeping popularity with the people of Kyōto.

Kabuki as it is today was originated in *"Kabuki* dance" performed by Izumo-no-Okuni. Originally, *Kabuki* dance was performed by young girls who disguised themselves as *samurai*. Later, in the Edo era, women were prohibited from appearing on the stage for the questionable reason that masquerading by females would seduce the public. This made it necessary for male actors to play roles of females. Since then, all parts in *Kabuki* drama have been played by men. The last known record about Izumo-no-Okuni goes that she performed a *Kabuki* dance before the second *shōgun* Tokugawa Hidetada in 1607.

THE PRE-MODERN AGE
◂‖ 近世 ‖▸

THE PRE-MODERN AGE

The two and a half centuries from 1603, when Ieyasu Tokugawa established the Edo shogunate in Edo (present-day Tokyo), through the Meiji Restoration (of Imperial rule) in 1867 are known as Japan's pre-modern age.

This unprecedented period of sustained peace and stability is attributed to a number of factors. One is the establishment of a strong political organization, with the ruling shogunate supported by faithful *daimyō* (regional land barons). Another involves efforts to sustain the domination of the warrior class through a social caste system, with the *samurai* at the top, followed by farmers, artisans and merchants. Also considered a key factor is the "closed country" policy adopted by the Tokugawa government, which was designed to prevent any interference in Japanese affairs by the nations of the West. This national isolation left Japan far behind the rest of the world in industry and other crucial areas, although it also provided the impetus for the cultivation of the *kabuki* theater, *ukiyoé* ("floating world painting") woodblock prints, and other indigenous forms of Japanese art and culture.

Japanese commerce began to flourish from the mid-Edo period on, with a merchant class steadily gaining strength in the big cities. Some merchants became so powerful that they went into the business of money lending to the shogunate or individual *daimyō,* and there came to be a saying that "Insulting an Ōsaka merchant can spell the downfall of a *daimyō.* " The lavish lifestyles of the shogunate and the *daimyō* added to their financial woes, and after over two centuries of peace the government at last began to lose its ability to rule effectively, with bribery and other corruption growing in scale and frequency.

In 1853 American gunboats arrived in Japanese waters, demanding that the nation open its doors to the rest of the world at once. The impact of this encounter cost the Tokugawa government the lasting vestiges of its leadership, and a trend of increasing social unrest ensued. The Meiji Restoration was both an "Imperial revolution" and a move toward modernization, with efforts directed toward realizing a new government capable of coping with the demands of the emerging new age. The Edo shogunate, which fought stubbornly to maintain the outdated values of the past, soon lost its ability to rule, and gradually collapsed.

TOKUGAWA IEYASU
徳川家康・1542—1616

It was Tokugawa Ieyasu that emerged as the final winner among a number of military heroes who had aimed at unifying the country in the Sengoku period. Born as the first son of a minor feudal lord of the Province of Mikawa (Aichi Prefecture) Ieyasu used his outstanding political talent and strategic ingenuity to establish the foundation of the Tokugawa era which lasted for more than 260 years.

The character of Tokugawa Ieyasu was aptly described by the following *haiku* poem:
"Na-ka-nu-na-ra Na-ku-ma-dé-ma-to-u Ho-to-to-gi-su"
(The cockoo doesn't sing? All right, I'll wait till it sings.)
While serving two masters — first Oda Nobunaga, then Toyotomi Hideyoshi, Ieyasu was staidly waiting for a chance to make himself master of the country.

Mikawa Province in which Ieyasu was born was situated between two major provinces: the province on the west was governed by the Imagawa family and the one on the east, by the Oda family. Ieyasu was held as hostage to the Oda family for two years since he was six years of age, and then to the Imagawa family for 12 years. The exceptional patience of Ieyasu was cultivated while he was spending his early days under such adverse circumstances.

The Battle of Sekigahara

In 1600, two years after the death of Toyotomi Hideyoshi, Tokugawa's 100,000-men army and Toyotomi's 80,000-men army led by Ishida Mitsunari fought a fierce battle at Sekigahara (Gifu Prefecture). It was literally the biggest civil war in Japanese history that divided the whole country into two parts. By winning this decisive war, Ieyasu could come to power as the first Tokugawa *Shōgun* — his long-cherished dream.

The *samurai* warriors of Mikawa Province fought bravely for Tokugawa Ieyasu. Legend has it that when they were defeated in a battle against Takeda Shingen, no one turned his back on the foe: all the dead warriors with their heads toward Hamamatsu (where Ieyasu's headquarters was placed) lay face up.

Ieyasu's victory in the Battle of Sekigahara was due to his successful tactics: he had previously made some feudal lords friendly to him join the Toyotomi army. The troops of Toyotomi which had the advantage in the early phase of the war began taking to flight as betrayers came out in succession from their side.

Even after the Battle of Sekigahara, Toyotomi Hideyori (son and heir of Hideyoshi) who was entrenching himself in the Osaka Castle was Ieyasu's most fearful political rival. Eventually, Ieyasu attacked the Ōsaka Castle under the pretext that he was offended by the lay-out of characters impressed on a temple bell cast on the order of Hideyori. His claim was that the two characters 家 (ie) and 康 (yasu) were set apart.

The Ōsaka Castle which Toyotomi Hideyoshi had built deliberately proved to be invincible even by a big force. So, Ieyasu made peace with Hideyori on condition that the outer moat of the castle be filled up with earth.

Ieyasu, however, filled up not only the outer moat but also the inner moat of the castle. Though built exceptionally strong, the Ōsaka Castle without moats became open to attack from outside.

In the following year, Ieyasu launched an all-out assault on the Ōsaka Castle. A fierce battle lasted for over a month. Eventually, the castle with its moats filled up collapsed. The Toyotomi family perished when Hideyori and his mother Yodogimi killed themselves in raging flames.

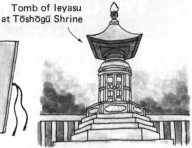

Tomb of Ieyasu
at Tōshōgū Shrine

When Ieyasu reached about 70, he began to transcribe the Buddhist invocation called *Namuamidabutsu* onto a scroll as long as 10 meters. It is said that he did that wishing to make amends for many lives he had deprived of in a number of battles.

Ieyasu died praying for prosperity of the Tokugawa family. Although eastern Japan was under control of feudal lords familiar with the Tokugawa family, there were still some feudal lords who had sided with the Toyotomi family in western Japan. Therefore, Ieyasu ordered to set the statue of god for his tomb toward the west.

Tokugawa Ieyasu is said to have left the following teachings on the conduct of life.

"Remember absolute satisfaction is denied to mortals, and you will be contented."

"Man's life is like walking a long way with a heavy load on his back. So, never hurry."

"Going too far is worse than falling a bit short."

TOKUGAWA IEMITSU

徳川家光・1604—1651

The Third Tokugawa *Shōgun* who succeeded the second *shōgun* Hidetada. By introducing *"sankin-kōtai"* (feudal lord's alternate-year attendance at the *shōgun*'s court) and *"hatamoto"* (*shōgun*'s direct vassal) systems, Tokugawa Iemitsu consolidated the Shogunate regime and brought the Shogunate to the peak of its power.

Torii (main gate) of the Tōshōgū Shrine

Iemitsu built a magnificent shrine called Tōshōgū at Nikkō in memory of his grandfather, Ieyasu.

When Iemitsu assumed the office of *shōgun,* he called feudal lords of various provinces to the Edo Castle and said to them, "I am born *shōgun.* I am not a friend to you. Neither do I owe my ascending the shogunate to you. Therefore, I will treat all of you as my vassals even if you were friends of my father (Hidetada) or grandfather (Ieyasu)."

TOKUGAWA TSUNAYOSHI
徳川綱吉・1646—1709

Fifth Tokugawa *Shōgun.* Tokugawa Tsunayoshi was the most unique in character among the fifteen Tokugawa shōguns. He showed such a fondness for living things, particularly canines, that he was called the "Dog *Shōgun.*" His reign is the so-called Genroku era. During this period, *chōnin* (the burghers) increased power significantly and the gay Genroku culture flourished, chiefly at Edo and Ōsaka.

Seidō

Tsunayoshi was fond of learning. He built a school named *"Seidō,"* where he himself occasionally lectured on confucianism.

According to tradition, Tsunayoshi treated dogs kindly because he was told by a priest that the reason why Tsunayoshi had been childless was that he had killed a dog in a previous incarnation. He inflicted severe punishment upon those who had killed or ill-treated a dog. Also, he made Shogunate officials build dog pounds, where stray dogs were given meals better than those taken by farmers those days.

In the first few years after Tsunayoshi became *shōgun,* he was fairly successful in his attempts to rebuild the financial strength of the Shogunate and improve social stability. Toward theend of his life, however, he indulged himself in a loose life, bringing about political chaos.

Eighth Tokugawa *Shōgun*. Tokugawa Yoshimuné managed to restore the prestige as well as the finances of the Shogunate. Along with Ieyasu and Iemitsu, Yoshimuné was exalted as an enlightened ruler. Since he was a realist and laid stress on practical knowledge, the study of European learning introduced into Japan by Dutch missionaries advanced remarkably during his reign.

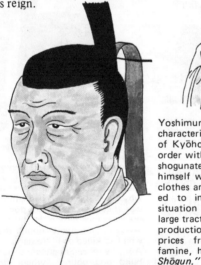
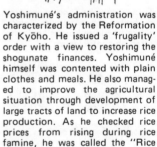

Yoshimuné's administration was characterized by the Reformation of Kyōho. He issued a 'frugality' order with a view to restoring the shogunate finances. Yoshimuné himself was contented with plain clothes and meals. He also managed to improve the agricultural situation through development of large tracts of land to increase rice production. As he checked rice prices from rising during rice famine, he was called the "Rice *Shōgun.*"

The Tokugawa Shogunate administration was highly characterized by continual efforts to consolidate financial bases. Following the Reformation of Kyōho, a number of reforms were carried out. However, since the finances of the shogunate had been based on agriculture, none of those reforms could be an effective solution to financial problems because they failed to make the most of the rising commerce.

Aoki Konyō

The most famous of various measures taken by Yoshimuné was the installation of "meyasu-bako." Meyasu-bako was a box into which townsmen could drop their suggestions as to the administration of political affairs or complaints about corrupt practices of government officials. Yoshimuné opened the boxes by himself so that he could reflect their opinion in his administration.

Yoshimuné lifted the ban on non-religious Western literature and thereby encouraged the study of European learning. Such liberal tone of society produced notable scholars such as Aoki Konyō who spread the cultivation of sweet potatoes to save farmers from starving during rice famine.

Tokugawa Yoshimuné was born of the Kii-han (Wakayama Prefecture), one of the three clans of the Tokugawa house. Since he was the fourth son, he was given only a small teritory. However, he became the head of the Kii clan when his father and elder brothers died in succession. Further, when Tokugawa Yoshimichi who was to succeed to the eighth shōgun died suddenly at the age of 25, Yoshimuné was appointed to the eighth shōgun.

The Tokugawa shogunate totally banned Christianity in 1612, burning Christians to death. In 1637, at Shimabara in Kyūshū, Christian farmers who had been groaning under heavy taxation raised a large-scale revolt. It was Amakusa Shirō, "son of God," that led the rebel army.

Amakusa Shirō was such a handsome boy that he was called a "son of God." There remain lots of legends about him: he broke a twig on which a bird perched, without touching the twig: a dove laid an egg in the palm of his hand; he walked on the sea; etc.

Christianity was introduced into Japan in the Sengoku period. Since then, the religion had been spread throughout the country, mainly in Kyūshū, by Catholic missionaries from Spain, Portugal, and other European countries. At Shimabara, which had once been governed by a Christian *daimyō* (feudal lord), Christianity was very popular among the farmers.

A feudal lord newly appointed by the Tokugawa shogunate imposed a heavy tax on the farmers and oppressed the Christians at Shimabara. According to legend, he let those who failed to pay taxes wear a straw coat and set fire thereto and thereby burned them to death. Such cruel oppression caused dissatisfaction of the farmers to mount.

It is said that when Amakusa Shirō raised a rebel army, more than 90% of the farmers joined voluntarily. The Tokugawa shogunate mobilized a 20,000-man army against the rebel army of some 37,000 men and women. However, the shogunate army failed to capture the fortress in which the rebels entrenched themselves. Besides, it lost its commander-in-chief during the fight.

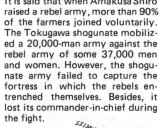

SSIM·SACRAMEN TO·

The shogunate then dispatched a big force of 120,000 soldiers with a view to suppressing the revolt. Yet, that big force could not heat the rebel army easily because the rebels remained closely united. Eventually, the shogunate army besieged the fortress and cut off the supply of food. Brought face to face with starvation, the rebels were strongly agitated to see Amakusa Shirō, whom they had believed as son of God, shot wounded. Taking this opportunity, the shogunate army launched an all-out assault on the fortress and suppressed the revolt. It is said that the captive farmers disobeyed the order "Abandon Christianity" and were beheaded with a smile on their face.

MIYAMOTO MUSASHI

宮本武蔵・？ー1645

Foremost swordsman of the Edo period. At the age of 13, Miyamoto Musashi left home to visit many provinces in order to train himself in swordsmanship. He was an unparalleled swordsman who registered 60 wins with no loss. The duel he fought with Sasaki Kojirō at Ganryūjima is very famous. In his later years, he wrote a book titled *"Gorin-no-sho"* which describes the soul of martial arts.

Long sword → · Short sword

Miyamoto Musashi originated a new style of fencing called *"nitō-ryū,"* in which he held a long sword in the right hand and a short one in the left hand.

In his *Gorin-no-sho,* Miyamoto Musashi notes that in order to master the art of fencing it is more important to train one's spirit than to improve his skill. He was also a talented painter as attested to by a number of his works full of vigor and refinement.

The Duel at Ganryūjima

Sasaki Kojirō was a prodigious swordsman who was said to be able to slash even a flying swallow. One day Musashi and Kojirō agreed to fight a duel on a small island called Ganryūjima.

On the day of the fight, Musashi intentionally deferred his departure for the island. On his way, Musashi shaped the scull of his boat into a long wooden sword.

Kept waiting for so long, Kojirō lost his composure. So, the moment Musashi landed ashore Kojirō struck at him. Musashi turned aside adroitly and pulled himself up in a fighting posture, with the shining sun on his back. Holding the wooden sword over his head, Musashi cried "Kojirō, you are lost!"

The fight was over in a matter of second when Musashi's wooden sword smashed Kojirō's forehead. Actually, the issue must have been decided when Kojirō was irritated by the late arrival of Musashi.

ŌISHI KURANOSUKÉ

大石蔵之助・1659—1703

Key vassal of the Akoo clan (Hyōgo Prefecture); real name, Ōishi Yoshio. Ōishi Kuranosuke is the most famous as the central figure in *"Chūshingura,"* the event in which he and his 45 comrades avenged their master, Asano Takuminokami, who had committed *hara-kiri* after slashing at Kira Kōzukenosuké, who was in an important office with the Tokugawa Shogunate.

The loyal retainers of Akoo lay in their graves at Sengaku-ji Temple in Minato Ward, Tōkyō. There, a grand festival called *"Gishi-matsuri"* is held on December 14 (the day on which they attained their aim) every year.

The story of Ōishi Kuranosuké and other loyal retainers of the Akoo clan was adopted for a *Kabuki* play and won exceptional popularity. Even today, this story of men having conquered many hardships to attain their aim charms many Japanese.

The Story of "Chūshingura"

Asano Takuminokami, lord of the Akoo clan, was appointed to the office of attending to envoys from the Imperial Court. He went to Kira Kōzukenosuké with a view to learning the etiquette and formality appropriate for his new office. Kōzukenosuké cried, "You, boorish *samurai*," and ignored his request.

In March 1701, becoming unable to bear repeated insult any longer, Asano Takuminokami slashed at Kōzukenosuké on the corridor in the Edo Castle. Takuminokami was held back by a chief vassal of the shogunate who happened to pass nearby. Kōzukenosuké got a scratch on the forehead.

In those days, wielding a sword within the Edo Castle was strictly prohibited. Since Asano Takuminokami violated the ban, he was ordered to commit *hara-kiri* and the territory of Akoo was confiscated, while Kira Kōzukenosuké was unpunished.

The vassals of the Akoo clan felt much dissatisfied with the judgment because "In a quarrel both parties shall be punished" was the rule of those days. Ōishi Kuranosuké who was entrusted with the management of the Akoo clan obediently surrendered the castle to the shogunate with the hope that some day the Asano house would be allowed to revive.

Up to that point, Ōishi Kuranosuke was considered a very ordinary man. He lived in Kyoto, and spent most of his time in the geisha houses of Gion. Because of his loose lifestyle, rumors that the retainers of the Ako clan would seek retaliation gradually died and people began to make fun of him.

In 1702, when it became clear that the prospect of revival of the Asano house was very little, 47 loyal retainers, including Kuranosuké and his son Ōishi Chikara, secretly gathered together at Edo with a view to avenging their master. (One of them dropped out immediately before they started for the vengeance.)

On the early morning of December 15, the 46 armed men raided on the residence of Kira in a heavy snowstorm. The scene of the men rushing into the residence at a signal with a drum beaten by Kuranosuké is called "Uchi-iri," the climax of Chūshingura.

Although they took possession of Kira's residence, they had great difficulty in finding out Kira. At last, one of the corps detected Kira Kōzukenosuké who was hiding himself in the charcoal burning shed, and cut off his head. Thus, the 46 loyal retainers of the Akoo clan avenged their master one year and nine months after he died resentfully.

Tomb of
Asano
Takuminokami

Kōzukenosuké's
head

From Kira's residence, they march- ed direct to Sengaku-ji Temple where their master Asano Takumi- nokami lay in his grave, and placed Kōzukenosuké's head before his tomb.

After the event, the Tokugawa Shogunate decided to temporarily keep the avengers in custody of the Hosokawa house, one of the major feudal lords. Deeply moved by the loyalty of Akoo's retainers, Hosokawa Tsunatoshi, head of the Hosokawa clan, asked the shogu- nate for their lives and at the same time, proposed that he took care of them as his vassals.

Tombs of the 46 men

On the other hand, there were those inside the shogunate who were insisting on punishing the avengers severely. They claimed that setting them free was admit- ting the previous shogunate's deci- sion as misjudgment and that any one who violated law should not remain unpunished.

Eventually, on February 4, 1703, all the loyal retainers who had participated in the vengeance were ordered to commit *hara-kiri*. Even today, Sengaku-ji Temple is fre- quented by people who pay homage to the 46 men lying in their graves there.

MITO MITSUKUNI

水戸光圀 · 1628—1700

Second lord of the Mito clan, one of the three branch families of the Tokugawa house. Known as a man of noble character, Mito Mitsukuni was adored not only by his vassals but also by the people in his territory. Fond of learning, he left a number of remarkable academic achievements. The most famous is *"Dai-Nihonshi,"* a voluminous book of Japanese history.

When Mitsukuni was six years of age, his father ordered him to bring the head of a beheaded criminal, with a view to testing his son's courage. Without showing any emotion at his father's weird command, Mitsukuni went to the execution ground and returned dragging a freshly-severed head.

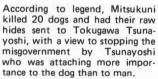

According to legend, Mitsukuni killed 20 dogs and had their raw hides sent to Tokugawa Tsunayoshi, with a view to stopping the misgovernment by Tsunayoshi who was attaching more importance to the dog than to man.

Mito Mitsukuni is more widely known for the rumor that after retirement he traveled around the country while punishing the wicked encountered on his way than for his actual life. The rumor almost everywhere goes as follows.

Mito Mitsukuni, followed by two men named "Suké-san" and "Kaku-san" is traveling in disguise through a certain province.

There appear poor farmers who they claim are ill-treated by a wicked local magistrate. Mitsukuni and his followers then decide to punish the local magistrate.

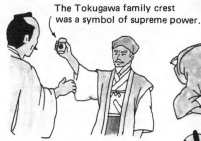

The Tokugawa family crest was a symbol of supreme power.

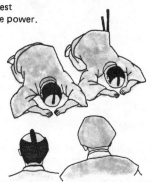

Entering the residence of the wicked magistrate, Mitsukuni holds up a small case carrying the crest of the Tokugawa house and the followers cry, "You see, this gentleman is the highly respectable vice-*shōgun*."

The villain and all his subordinates prostrate themselves on the spot and apologize to our hero.

ŌOKA TADASUKE
大岡忠相・1677—1751

Edo machi-bugyō (commissioner of town administration) of the middle Edo period. Selected to *Edo machi-bugyō* by the eighth *shōgun* Tokugawa Yoshimuné, Ōoka Tadasuké was admired for his invariably fair judgments. His remarkable administrative achievements have been exalted in *"rakugo"* (comic storytelling) and *Kabuki* drama.

Ōoka Tadasuké lies in his grave at Jōken-ji Temple in Kanagawa Prefecture, which was formerly included in his territory.

Owing to his distinguished services, Ōoka Tadasuké was ultimately promoted to a feudal lord. Since he started as a low-level official, it was an exceptional promotion in those days.

The criminal law of those days was highly characterized by severeness. For example, if one member of a family committed a crime, not only the criminal but also his (or her) parents and other members of the family were punished. Ōoka Tadasuké applied that joint-liability punishment system only to parricide or murder of one's master, and prohibited abuse of torture. He also made positive efforts to revise the excessively rigid criminal law.

Most of the stories told about Ōoka Tadasuké are fictions made after his death. Those fictions, however, reflect that the people of those days eagerly wanted fair judges.

One day, Tadasuké saw two women struggling for a child. Since each of them kept saying that she was the child's true mother, he declared, "You, two women, pull the child's hands at the same time, one from this side and the other from that side. The party having pulled the child away from the other shall be held as the real mother."

As his hands were pulled from both sides, the child began crying with pain. At that moment, one of the women let his hand go involuntarily. Tadasuké now ordered this woman to take the child, saying to the other woman, "If you were the child's true mother, you must have let his hand go as he was crying with pain."

Gold coin one ryō

Another day, Tadasuké encountered two men who were disputing over the ownership of three ryō (unit of old Japanese coinage). He then picked one ryō out of his purse and handed it to them, saying, "You, take two ryō each." His logic of fairness was this. Every party involved suffered a loss of one ryō!

三方一両損

YAMADA NAGAMASA

山田長政・？—1630

In the beginning of the seventeenth century, Japanese towns mushroomed at various parts of Southeast Asia — the Philippines, Thailand, Vietnam, etc. Most of those towns were settled by Christians expatriated from Japan and *samurai* warriors of the Toyotomi army defeated in the Battle of Sekigahara. Yamada Nagamasa who led the bodyguards of the King of Thailand was one of those Japanese who sought a new field of activity overseas.

It is said that Nagamasa died in agony because someone who had envy of his fame applied deadly poison over a wound Nagamasa got in the leg during a battle.

According to legend, Yamada Nagamasa was a palanquin-bearer of Suruga Province (Shizuoka Prefecture). After he crossed the sea to Siam (Thailand), he became the mayor of a Japanese town. Heading some 800 Japanese soldiers, he joined the bodyguards of the King of Siam. Nagamasa and his subordinates won much confidence of the King. After the King died, however, Nagamasa was put out of the capital and lived his last few years as governor of .... (central part of the Malay peninsula).

NAKAHAMA MANJIRŌ
中浜万次郎・1827—1898

Fisherman of Tosa Province (Kōchi Prefecture). In 1841, his ship was wrecked in a storm and Manjiro was thrown ashore of an uninhabited islet. Eventually, he was rescued by the crew of a U.S. whaleboat. Given an American name "John Man," he spent some 10 years in Hawaii, New York, and other parts of the United States. After he returned home, he made significant contribution to the Meiji Restoration by spreading new knowledge he had obtained in the New World.

Nakahama Manjirō was the first Japanese that landed on a Western country after Japan closed the door to foreigners in 1639.

The captain of the whaleboat liked Manjiro so much that he decided to take this Japanese boy to his home town in New York. There Manjirō learned English for two years.

At the age of 19, Manjiro joined the crew of a whaleboat to sail around the world. Being a competent sailor, he was ultimately promoted to assistant captain. After he left the boat, he worked in a gold mine in California in order to make money for his returning home.

When Manjirō returned to Japan, which was still in national isolation, he was subjected to thoroughgoing examination by the shogunate. After two years of strict surveillance by the authorities, he was treated as one of few Japanese who were well informed of overseas affairs. He then played an active part in the fields of translation and interpretation. He also became professor of a university.

KINOKUNIYA BUNZAEMON

紀伊国屋文左衛門・1669—1734

Business tycoon of the Edo period. Kinokuniya Bunzaemon made a vast fortune by transporting a huge amount of mandarin oranges over a stormy sea to the markets in Edo. After that, he became a merchant under shogunate patronage to enjoy the reputation of a businessman with political affiliations. Because of his exceptionally extravagant merry-making, he was called *"Kibun Daijin"* (Kinokuniya Bunzaemon, seeker of riotous pleasures).

The then Edo was so densely populated and packed with so many wooden houses that it witnessed a big fire many times. In fact, such a devastating fire that destroyed most of the towns of Edo occurred more than 20 times. Such being the case, most business tycoons of those days were timber traders. Kinokuniya Bunzaemon was one of those timber traders.

Matoi—fireman's standard

The expression "The Tokyoite will not keep his earnings overnight," sometimes used to represent the cheerful optimism (or pessimism) of the inhabitants of Tōkyō reminds us of the fact that a big fire was almost a daily occurrence in the former Tōkyō (Edo).

114

Mandarin oranges

The mandarin orange is indispensable to the Japanese for celebrating *"Shōgatsu"* (New Year's Day). In a certain year, the supply of mandarin oranges to Edo was almost cut off by stormy weather. Then, the prices of mandarin oranges started to skyrocket at Edo, while those in the orange-producing districts began declining sharply.

Paying attention to that peculiar situation, Kinokuniya Bunzaemon recruited 20 foolhardy sailors at generous wages and let them carry huge amounts of mandarin oranges over a raging sea to Edo. Bunzaemon thus became a billionaire overnight.

The residence of Kinokuniya Bunzaemon was as large as a town block. He had all *tatami* (straw mats) replaced every day, so that any of his guests never sat on the same *tatami* on his second visit.

On the evening of February 3, people scatter roasted soybeans inside and outside their homes to expel evil spirits. It is said that Kinokuniya Bunzaemon scattered gold coins instead of roasted soybeans.

ISHIKAWA GOEMON

石川五右衛門・1558?—1594?

According to traditional belief, Ishikawa Goemon was a benevolent robber of the Azuchi-Momoyama period. When his attempt to assassinate Toyotomi Hideyoshi failed, Goemon was sentenced to death by boiling in a cauldron. Later, in the Edo era, the life of Goemon as a Robin Hood was dramatized in *Kabuki* and *Jōruri* plays, making him popular among the general public.

Boiled water

When Ishikawa Goemon was put in the cauldron, together with his small child, he held his child above the boiling water till he himself was boiled to death.

In the climactic scene of the notable *Kabuki* play *"Sanmon Gosanno-Kiri,"* the hero, Ishikawa Goemon, cries "What a grand sight!" from atop the towering main gate *(Sanmon)* of Nanzen-ji Temple at Kyōto.

NEZUMI KOZŌ
鼠小僧・？—1832

Thief who acted in Edo in the 1820's. Since Nezumi Kozō broke into only rich men's residences in an audacious way, the general public felt refreshed by his act. He was captured and executed in 1832. Later, he was taken up as the hero in various *Kabuki* plays, novels, and dramas.

The name "Nezumi Kozō" (literal ly, mouse boy) was given to this consummate thief because he was dressed in black and nimbly moved from one roof to another, giving his pursuers a slip under cover of the night.

Nezumi Kozō became a hero among the general mass when the rumor spread that he distributed the money he had stolen from feudal lords and rich merchants to poor men's homes without being noticed by anyone. Actually, how ever, he spent all the money he had stolen in gambling and *saké*-drinking.

117

IHARA SAIKAKU
井原西鶴・1642—1693

Novelist of the Edo period. Born in the Genroku era characterized by ripe culture, Ihara Saikaku vividly described various aspects of the life of the newly arisen merchant class and thereby established a new genre of novels called *"Ukiyo-zōshi"* (literally, novels of the floating world). Along with Chikamatsu Monzaemon (*"Jōruri"* playwright) and Matsuo Bashō (*"Haiku"* composer), Ihara Saikaku was one of the literary giants of the Edo period.

Ihara Saikaku was born of a wealthy merchant in Ōsaka. When he was 33 years of age, he lost his wife. He then transferred his store to the clerk and started literary career. He learned *haiku* first. At that time, he composed 23,500 *haiku* in a day, surprising the company with his unique talent.

Most of the works of Ihara Saikaku deal with the merchant class and money: *"Kōshoku Ichidai-Otoko"* depicting love affairs of townsmen of the merchant class; *"Nihon Eitaigura,"* a collection of success stories of merchants whose purpose of life was money-making; *"Seken Munazanyō"* describing the lives of poor townsmen having difficulty in securing daily bread; etc. His unique style and sense of humor had no small influence on modern Japanese literature.

TAKIZAWA BAKIN
滝沢馬琴・1767—1848

Novelist of the Edo period. Takizawa Bakin is known as the author of *"Nansō Satomi Hakkenden,"* a 106-volume novel which took him 28 years to complete. He was a first-class entertainment writer who fascinated the readers by his intriguing plan and elegant style.

Fusé-himé

Miracle dog Yatsufusa

While he was writing *"Nansō Satomi Hakkenden,"* he lost the sight of his right eye and then lost his son. At the age of 73, he lost the sight of the other eye and met the death of his wife. Yet, kindled with the passion for his lifework, he at last completed the novel by dictating the remaining portion to his son's wife.

Nansō Satomi Hakkenden
The story begins when the virgin Fusé-hime, daughter of the lord of the Satomi house flourishing in the Muromachi period, becomes pregnant as she is molested by the evil spirit of witch dog *"Yatsufusa."* In order to prove her innocence, she kills herself, when eight beads of her rosary scatter and turn into eight brave men. They fight a fierce struggle with the witch who has taken over the Satomi house, and eventually, they reinstate the Satomi house. This novel with more than 300 characters is the masterpiece embodying Bakin's whole mental and physical energy.

CHIKAMATSU MONZAEMON
近松門左衛門・1653—1724

Dramatist of the Edo period. With a keen eye on the fully-matured culture of townsmen of the Genroku era, Chikamatsu Monzaemon wrote many excellent plays for *Kabuki* and *Jōruri* (puppet play). He is well known as the first Japanese dramatist who introduced a dramatic framework into the traditional stage arts which had been highly dependent on the accomplishments of individual actors. It is said that he is the greatest dramatist Japan has ever had.

Jōruri is a kind of puppet play in which puppets are manipulated to a story told with a peculiar intonation by a performer called *"tayū."* It was established as a popular art in the Edo period.

Chikamatsu Monzaemon was highly successful in his attempts to take up contemporary social phenomena, especially a double suicide, as his themes for *Jōruri* which had been dealing almost exclusively with past events. His contemporary plays called *"sewa-mono"* vividly depict the everyday life and sentiments of townsmen of the Edo period.

Samurai
Farmer
Craftsman
Merchant
Outcasts

Chikamatsu Monzaemon was born of a poor *samurai* family. When he entered into the world of popular arts, the people around him were much surprised because in the hierarchical society of the Edo era, the *samurai* class was placed at the top, while actors (called outcasts) were placed at the bottom.

One day, his younger brother, who was a doctor, said to Monzaemon, "I wish you would stop writing books for trifling *jōruri.*" To this Monzaemon answered, "The slightest mistake in the writing of a medical book can be fatal. That's not the case with my books."

In the Genroku era which saw a remarkable growth of commerce, money trouble was a frequent occurrence. Also, in this era, *"giri"* (loyalty to one's patron) was regarded as the highest moral of merchants. More often than not, *"giri"* prevented young lovers from getting married to each other. Under such circumstances, a double suicide occurred frequently.

"Sonezaki Shinjū," which made Monzaemon famous, was written on the basis of an actual case of double suicide. It provides a very realistic representation of the process of a young couple coming to choose a double suicide as their final solution to the dilemma between girl and money. Even today, this story is played on the *Kabuki* stage, attracting many spectators.

MATSUO BASHŌ
松尾芭蕉・1644—1694

Haiku poet of the Edo period. Matsuo Bashō brought *haiku* from a mere passtime of townsmen up to the level of an art in which the beauty and richness of the Japanese language are sought. He spent most of his lifetime traveling round the country. After practicing rigorous self-discipline, he established aesthetics of his own. Admired as *"Hai-sei" (haiku* master), Matsuo Bashō is one of the greatest literary figures of Japan.

Matsuo Bashō studied *haiku* in a humble cottage called *"Bashō-an."* The name *"Bashō"* was taken from *'bashō'* (Japanese name of plantain) planted in the garden of his cottage.

Bashō-an at Fukagawa, Kōtō Ward, Tōkyō

Haiku is probably the world's shortest form of poetry consisting of only 17 syllables in five-seven-five pattern. Bashō found the infinite in this form of poem reduced to possible limit. One of his masterpieces is this.

"Fu-ru-i-ké-ya Ka-wa-zu-to-bi-ko-mu Mi-zu-no-o-to"
(A frog jumped in an old pond, breaking the silence which had reigned all round.)

Bashō

At the age of 45, Bashō, together with one of his pupils, started for a long journey round the northeastern part of Honshū (main island), for he had long thought of life in terms of a journey. *"Oku-no-Hosomichi,"* a collection of his most famous *haiku*, was a precious souvenir from Bashō.

Minatogawa, old battlefield

When Bashō visited the place where he was told Minamoto-no-Yoshitsuné had died, he shed tears for the sad fate of Yoshitsuné and his followers. There Bashō composed the following famous *haiku:* *"Na-tsu-ku-sa-ya Tsu-wa-mo-no-do-mo-ga Yu-me-no-a-to*

Summer grass.
The dreams of great warriors
Are all that remain.

Bashō and his companion once stopped in a wretched inn where they had to sleep on a thin straw mat laid over dirt floor. Annoyed by fleas and mosquitoes, Bashō could hardly sleep. Worse still, his chronic disease, chololithiasis, tormented him so severely that he almost fainted. However, he never stayed in the same place because he wished to die while traveling.

Rakushi-sha in Kyoto

In his evening years, Bashō frequented the house called *Rakushi-sha.* His death *haiku* poem was this. *"Ta-bi-ni-yan-de Yu-me-wa-ka-re-no-o Ka-ke-me-gu-ru"*

Sick on a journey.
My dreams wander on
Across a desolate plain.

Bashō composed this *haiku* just before he died from food poisoning on his way to Kyūshū.

Haiku poet of the Edo period. Born of a poor farmer in Shin-shū (Nagano Prefecture), he left home for Edo at the age of 14. In Edo, he led a hard life as an apprentice. In his unique style characterized by the use of slangs and dialects, he composed many *haiku* poems expressing his compassion for the weak and antipathy against the strong. Even today, his works full of human tenderness are loved by many Japanese.

You have no parents like me...

When Issa was two years of age, his mother died. Thereafter, he was brought up by his father and grandmother. When Issa was eight years old, his father remarried. The stepmother treated him harshly. So, it is said, Issa used to feel society in sparrows and other small living things he could watch in the garden.

Lonely Issa in the stonehouse

At the age of 51, Issa returned home and got married. His four children had a weak constitution and passed away in succession. His wife died when Issa was 62. It is said that after his house was destroyed by fire he used to confine himself in his storehouse.

Issa composed more than 20,000 *haiku* in his lifetime. Almost all of them were associated with the joy and sorrow of poor people in their lives.

JIPPENSHA IKKU
十返舎一九・1765-1831

Comic-book writer of the Edo period. Son of a low-rank official of Sunpu Province (Shizuoka Prefecture), he wandered about the country. At the age of 37, he wrote a comic book titled *"Tōkaidō-chū Hizakurigé,"* which gained sweeping popularity all over Edo.

Yajirobei   Kitahachi

"Tōkaidō-chū Hizakurigé" describes, in an amusing way, the journey of two heroes, *"Yajirobei"* and *"Kitahachi,"* on the *Tōkaidō* highway from Edo (later Tōkyō) to Ōsaka. Probably because of exceptional popularity it won, Ikku wrote one continuation after another for 21 years, making the two heroes travel around the whole country.

Ikku was good at calligraphy and painting, as well as writing novels. However, he was a man of moods and in his last years, he became addicted to drinking and led an unhappy life.

After the death of Ikku, the rumor spread that at his funeral he astonished the attendants by letting a fire-cracker which he had concealed in his bosom crack during the cremation.

BOMB!

KANŌ TANYŪ
狩野探幽 · 1602—1674

Painter of the early Edo period. Grandson of the artistic genius Kanō Eitoku of the Momoyama period (known for his grand, pompous style), Kanō Tanyū was good at unconventional black-and-white paintings. Thanks to the advent of Kanō Tanyū, the Kanō school of painting came to enjoy an enormous popularity in the Edo period.

Part of "*Kinkisho-ezu*," one of Tanyū's masterpieces.

Kanō Tanyū started painting at the age of four. At 13, he drew a picture of a cat before the *shōgun*, who admiringly said that he (Tanyū) was like another Kanō Eitoku.

The Kanō school had continued to have unrivaled influence on Japanese paintings from the Muromachi period through the Meiji period. The founder of the Kanō school was Kanō Masanobu, a painter in the employ of the *shōgun* Ashikaga Yoshimasa of the Muromachi shogunate. The school was firmly established by his grandson, Kanō Eitoku, who drew superb wall paintings for the Azuchi Castle of Oda Nobunaga and the Ōsaka Castle and Juraku-dai Mansion of Toyotomi Hideyoshi.

OGATA KŌRIN
尾形光琳・1658—1716

Painter and craftsman of the Genroku (Edo) period. Second son of a wealthy dry-goods dealer in Kyōto, he became the most popular painter of the Genroku era for his bold and decorative style. He was also known as a highly-gifted craftsman. Together with his younger brother, Ogata Kenzan, he left a number of superb paintings on scrolls.

Part of *"Kōbai-hakubai-zu"*

Ogata Kōrin was especially good at screen paintings of flowering plants. He also left many excellent black-and-white paintings and narrative paintings characterized by unconventionality. The unique pattern on *kimono* worked out by him was called *"Kōrin pattern,"* which enjoyed great popularity for a long time.

Painter of the Edo period. He preferred to depict manners of townsmen of Edo, actors on stage, and beautiful women. As he offered his paintings in the form of low-cost wood-block prints, *"ukiyoé"* (pictures depicting the life of worldly joys) became very popular among the general public.

"Mikaeri Bijin" one of Moronobu's masterpieces

Wood-block prints of those days were produced in a simple process: The painter draws a design, the engraver carves the design in a wood-block, then the printer produces copies of the design by applying paper to the carved wood-block to which black ink is previously applied. Other colors were added to wood-block prints as required using a brush.

KITAGAWA UTAMARO
喜多川歌磨・1753—1806

Notable *ukiyoé* painter. Not contented with the traditional style of painting beautiful women which sought women's beauty in their particular poses or attire, he originated *"Ōkubié"* (painting of the head and shoulders of a woman). His style of painting *ukiyoé* which sought feminine charms in woman countenances predominated in the *ukiyoé* world of the day. Along with Tōshūsai Sharaku famous for his paintings of *Kabuki* actors, Katsushika Hokusai famous for his landscape paintings, Utamaro was one of the foremost *ukiyoé* painters.

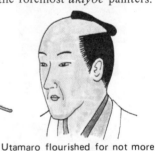

Utamaro flourished for not more than six years. Thereafter, he lost his original spirit and left only mediocre works. At 51, he drew a painting of Toyotomi Hideyoshi drinking *saké* surrounded by beautiful ladies. As this painting was criticized as a satire against the *shōgun's* lifestyle, he was put in jail. He died of illness at 53.

In his days, *ukiyoé* was otherwise called *"nishikié"* (color print) because most *ukiyoé* were painted in more than 10 gay colors. Utamaro, however, preferred to use less colors so as to improve the coloring effect. He also used a number of novel techniques. For example, he was highly successful in his attempt to impart a special effect to the background.

Notable *ukiyoé* artist of the Edo period. He drew facial expressions of *Kabuki* actors in bold deformation with superb constructive capacity and dynamism. Though he is today reckoned among world-famous portrait painters, his life is completely shrouded in mystery.

The only fact known of him is that he made 140 works in the 10 months from May 1794 to February 1795. Thus, he made his sudden appearance from the shadows of history, presented the world with lots of *ukiyoé* masterpieces, and disappeared in the darkness as suddenly as he had appeared.

It seems that Sharaku's unique style was little appreciated by the people of the day. As a matter of fact, it was in Europe, not Japan, that his works won fame first.

KATSUSHIKA HOKUSAI
葛飾北斎・1760—1849

Notable *ukiyoé* artist of the late Edo period. He is famous especially for *"Fugaku Sanjūrokkei,"* a set of 36 landscape paintings of Mt. Fuji. His style was characterized by bold composition and impressive presentation with a touch of European style. He had no small influence on French impressionists.

According to legend, Hokusai on his deathbed said, "I want to live at least five years more. If I could, I'd show you what the 'true' painting is like." At that time, he was 89 years old and had already released more than 30,000 works. Thus he devoted all his life to painting pictures.

Hokusai was known as a man of eccentric conduct (throughout his life he changed his abode 98 times!). A lot of amusing anecdotes were told of him: When his house was on fire, he escaped with nothing but a paint-brush in his hand; he used to walk along the street chanting the Buddhist invocation in order to prevent himself from being involved in time-wasting chat with a friend on the street.

SAKAIDA KAKIEMON

酒井田柿右衛門・1596—1666

Notable potter of the Edo period. He was the first potter who succeeded in creating exquisite porcelain called *"Akaé."* The name "Kakiemon" was given him by a feudal lord who was deeply impressed by the elaborate ornamental persimmon (*'kaki'* in Japanese) worked out by Sakaida. This honorable name has been handed down from generation to generation. Today the 13th Kakiemon is playing an active part in this field.

Teabowl
created by Kakiemon

"Akaé" is ceramic ware colored red, green, yellow, etc. The *akaé* works of Kakiemon were characterized by Japanese elegance created by a *Kanō*-style painting in vivid colors leaving much of the lustrous milky-white color as the background. Not a few of his works were exported to South Asia and Europe, exerting much influence on the potteries in their localities.

In those days, blue was the only color that could technically be reproduced on porcelain. One day Kakiemon was strikingly affected at the sight of ripe persimmons in his garden shining brilliant red in the splendor of the setting sun. He then made up his mind to reproduce that red on ceramics. He had spent nearly 20 years and all his money in his attempts to reproduce that red when he succeeded in creating exquisite *akaé* at the age of 50.

132

ICHIKAWA DANJŪRŌ
市川団十郎・1660—1704

Kabuki actor of the early Edo period. He swayed the minds of *Kabuki* fans by originating unique facial makeup with red and black paints and exaggerated movements called *ara-goto*. The Ichikawa house, of which he was a member, is a leading family of the *Kabuki* circle, and has produced many superb *Kabuki* actors.

Kumadori—Special makeup of *Kabuki*

Ichikawa Danjūrō devoted his life to the *Kabuki* drama. When he was 45 years of age, however, he was stabbed to death in his dressing room by a *Kabuki* actor who had envy of his fame.

The name "Ichikawa Danjūrō" is a hereditary name for the family's head and star actor of *Kabuki*. The man introduced here was the first Ichikawa Danjūrō. Today's star actor is the 12th Ichikawa Danjūrō.

Another prominent *Kabuki* actor who shared exceptional fame with Ichikawa Danjūrō in Edo was Sakata Tōjūrō in Kyōto. In contrast to masculine Danjūrō, Tōjūrō excelled in playing the role of a handsome young man having somewhat feminine touch.

SANYŪTEI ENCHŌ

三遊亭円朝・1839—1900

Raconteur of comic stories who flourished between the late Edo period and the early Meiji period. He excelled in comic storytelling in a dramatic setup with original costume, makeup, background, and stage effect. In his later years, he wrote *"Botandōrō"* and many other notable stories for himself. Even today, his prominent accomplishments in the art of storytelling have great influence on many of the raconteurs of comic stories.

Enchō's father was an entertainer, who was so loose a man that his family was faring poor. Therefore, at the age of 7, Enchō was already singing songs on the stage to earn petty money.

Since Enchō's stage was attractively gay, he won overwhelming popularity with young women. In the early Meiji period, he was as popular as present-day TV stars.

In his late years, Enchō, with nothing but a folding fan in his hand, charmed the audience with his narration and small gestures alone, and thereby brought comic storytelling up to the level of art.

NINOMIYA SONTOKU
二宮尊徳・1787—1856

Agricultural administrator of the Edo period. Otherwise called Ninomiya Kinjirō. Son of a poor farmer, he pursued knowledge under difficulties to become an authority on farm management. He played a vital role in restoring the farms and finances for the Odawara clan. Throughout his life, he visited more than 600 farm villages to improve the life of farmers.

In his boyhood, Sontoku used to read a book while carrying a fagot on his back. He was then under the care of his uncle, since he had lost his parents and his family's farm had been flooded into wasteland. So, it was his dream to make money to buy a new farm and recall his younger brothers to the farm, and thereby restore the Ninomiya house.

Sontoku was a polite, laborious man faithful to his parents. He preached diligence and saving, and stressed that public interest should be given priority over private interest. This thought of his was abused by prewar nationalists in their campaigns.

HIRAGA GENNAI
平賀源内・1726—1779

Scholar of the middle Edo period. Son of a poor *samurai* of the Takamatsu clan (Kagawa Prefecture), he learned Dutch at Nagasaki to study natural history and pharmacology. Having profound learning and great ability, he was a natural scientist, inventor, European-style painter, novelist, and playwright. However, he could not attain to greatness in any of those fields and led an unhappy life.

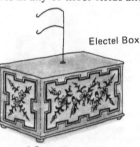

Electel Box

Some of Gennai's inventions
* Electel (hand-operated dynamo)
* Thermometer
* Asbestos cloth fabrication process
* Woolen cloth fabrication process

As Gennai failed in his efforts to exploit a mine for more than 10 years, he was labeled as humbug. Since his unusual ideas and gadgets were not appreciated by the people of the day, he used to satisfy his resentment by writing a novel or drama in his later years. He died in despair in the jail in which he had been put on the charge that he had struck at his assistant with a sword.

SUGITA GENPAKU
杉田玄白・1733—1817

Doctor of the late Edo period. Without the help of a Dutch dictionary, he translated "Tarhel Anatomia" (Dutch book on anatomy) in three years, and published his translation under the title "Kaitai Shinsho." He was a pioneer in modern Japanese medicine.

Shown here is the picture on the front cover of "Kaitai Shinsho," Japan's first translation of European medical book. After the publication of Kaitai Shinsho,, Japanese medicine made a rapid progress.

Cover of the Kaitai Shinsho

A few people helped Genpaku translate the book. However, since they had not a Dutch dictionary and knew only some 700 Dutch terms, the work progressed at a snail's pace: there were days when not a single line could be translated.

When Genpaku was 38 years of age, he had an opportunity to observe a human anatomical dissection which had been banned in those days. It is said that he made up his mind to translate the Dutch book on anatomy when he found that the book had an illustration showing the interior of a human body which was exactly the same as that he observed for the first time.

MOTOORI NORINAGA
本居宣長・1730—1801

Japanese classical scholar of the Edo period. He is noted for his 44-volume *"Kojikiden,"* a commentary to the Japanese classic *"Kojiki*,"* completed in 35 years. In his book, Norinaga dared to denounce the traditional criticism on *"Kojiki"* and sought unbiased literary value in that history book. At the same time, he discussed nationalism in the light of Japanese classical literature and expelled ideas borrowed from abroad, and thereby he contributed much to the development of national literature.

Bell →

It is said that Norinaga had three dozens of small bells hung on a pillar of his study, which he sounded to ease the fatigue from reading. Hence his home was called *"Suzunoya"* (literally, bell-house).

In his youth, Norinaga assiduously studied Japanese classics while practicing pediatrics. He made up his mind to write *"Kojikiden"* when he met the famous classics scholar Kamo-no-Mabuchi, who said to Norinaga, "I grow much old while studying *"Manyōshu*."* I would like you to study *"Kojiki"* in place of me."

Young Norinaga Kamo-no-Mabuchi

INŌ TADATAKA
伊能忠敬 · 1745—1818

Geographer of the Edo period. At the age of 50, he started learning astronomical chronology and surveying. In the 17 years from the age of 55, he completed a map of all Japan based on actual measurement. This map called *"Inō-zu"* was Japan's first accurate map prepared by using modern surveying technology.

Inō-zu
It admirably compares with the present-day map of Japan.

Ryōtei-sha

Shown here is the device called *"ryōtei-sha"* Tadataka used for land surveying. It automatically gives the distance as it is drawn on the road.

Though Tadataka showed a brilliant talent in mathematics from his childhood, he had to suspend his learning career because his family was too poor to afford it. When he was 18, he was adopted into the Ino house, local *saké*-maker and big landlord. There he worked hard to revive the once sluggish *saké* business. When he reached 50, he retired to resume learning.

SHIMIZU-NO-JIROCHŌ
清水次郎長・1820—1893

Big boss of *yakuza* (gangsters) who flourished between the late Edo period and the early Meiji period*. Son of a ferryman of Shimizu Port in Shizuoka Prefecture, Jirocho built up a big force of *yakuza* for himself. In the Meiji era, his syndicate was entrusted with civil-engineering works and marine transportation by the government.

Storyteller

Shimizu-no-Jirochō was an un-usually audacious, yet humane, boss who was adored by his followers. The syndicate's perform-mance became widely known when they were taken up in popu-lar novels, etc.

Mori-no-Ishimatsu
One of Jirocho's subordinates. According to traditional belief, he was a quick-to-quarrel, simple, good-natured, maudlin man. It is said that he was taken his life by stratagem and avenged by Jirochō who grew mad at his death.

THE MODERN AGE

◀‖近代‖▶

THE MODERN AGE

The Meiji period (the region of the Meiji Emperor from 1868 through 1912) was an age of great struggle for Japan, as it moved to transform itself from a feudal state into a modern capitalist nation. The government enacted a constitution, established a diet, and introduced other measures designed to create a modern political organization. In reality, however, the Emperor held power, with the Diet serving largely as his auxiliary organ. The military forces were also placed under Imperial control, with the Emperor at the center of the national mechanism.

Under this rule, the government set its sights on national prosperity and defense, encouraging Japanese industry to catch up with its U.S. and European counterparts, and introducing a conscription system to boost the strength of its military. The Meiji period was also characterized by victories in conflicts with China and Russia and the acquiring of Japan's first colonies, as the nation took its first steps down the road of imperialism.

During the Taishō period (the reign of the Taishō Emperor from 1912 through 1926), World War I provided a boon to Japanese exports and trade, boosting national strength to an unprecedented level. However, this postwar business prosperity was short-lived, and with the recovery of European industry the volume of Japanese exports dropped, triggering economic depression. This downward trend was aggravated in 1923 when the Kanto region was struck by a devastating earthquake, with massive destruction suffered in much of Tōkyō and the surrounding region.

In the early days of the Shōwa period (the reign of Emperor

Hirohito from 1926 to the present), the United States, which had prospered from the effects of World War I, fell into a grave economic depression (touched off by the stock market crash of 1929) which soon became global in scale. The Japanese economy was also hard hit by this depression, and the nation attempted to weather the hard times through colonization of the Chinese continent. In time, America, Great Britain, France and Russia came to China's aid, largely isolating Japan from the international community. Japan responded with a massive invasion of China under the pretext of "the liberation of Asia from the West," setting the scene for the nightmarish Pacific War with the United States and its allies.

With the end of World War II in 1945, Japan lay in total defeat, with much of her cities and industry reduced to ashes. However, backed by the combination of American support and Japanese diligence, the nation achieved an unprecedented recovery, rising to its current status as an economic superpower only a few decades after resounding defeat.

As the only nation ever to experience the horrors of nuclear bombing, Japan enacted the world's first "peace constitution," based on the renunciation of all acts of war.

Yet today Japan is certainly not without its critics, both domestic and overseas, and the demands for Japanese capital and technology to aid in the development in Asia, Africa and other developing regions continue to grow in intensity.

The postwar years have seen Japan rise to a position of major economic and political importance in the global order, and there is little doubt that its role in promoting world peace and prosperity will continue to grow from here on.

EMPEROR MEIJI
明治天皇・1852—1912

122nd Emperor. He ascended the throne at the age of 15. When he was 17, the Meiji Revolution* took place, bringing political power back to the Emperor after the lapse of some seven centuries from the end of the Heian period. During his 45-year reign, Japan won two big wars (Sino-Japanese and Russo-Japanese), thereby emerging as a modern nation. As a result, he came to be called the Great Emperor Meiji.

The Emperor Meiji displayed his political ability wonderfully: He promulgated a modern constitution and convened a national assembly for the first time in Asia.

Meiji-jingu Shrine at Harajuku, Tōkyō is dedicated to the Emperor Meiji. It receives many people for the first visit of the New Year.

A total of 76 conferences were held to compile the Meiji Constitution (the Japanese Imperial Constitution), the document which formed the base for Japan's emergence as a modern nation state. The Meiji Emperor was present at every one of these meetings.

Last (15th) *shōgun* of the Tokugawa shogunate. With the aid of the French government, he took a number of drastic measures to maintain the Tokugawa shogunate. However, when he found it impossible to stem the rushing wave of the Meiji Revolution*, he resigned from the shogunate, thereby putting an end to the reign of the Tokugawa house which lasted for more than 260 years.

Shōgun! Where are you going?

Recognized as a man of talent from his childhood, he was said to be another Tokugawa Ieyasu. He was, however, somewhat capricious and small-hearted. Therefore, he threw off the shogunate as soon as he saw the general situation was against him.

When the emperor's army seized Edo, Yoshinobu was confining himself in Kan'ei-ji Temple at Ueno. Since he had continued to be obedient to the Meiji government, he was eventually endowed with the title of Prince by the Emperor.

After his resignation from the shogunate, a rebellion was raised by vassals of the Tokugawa shogunate (Battle of *Toba-Fushimi*). On that occasion, he fled alone on a warship back to Edo while pretending to command the rebel army.

Kan'ei-ji Temple

145

KATSU KAISHŪ
勝海舟・1823—1899

Vassal of the *shōgun* of the Edo period and statesman of the early Meiji period. He learned European military science from Dutchmen. At the age of 37, he crossed the Pacific to San Francisco on the *Kanrin-maru* (warship) as the ship's captain. After he returned home, he helped the shogunate build an armed sea force. After the Meiji government was formed, he displayed superb talent as a statesman.

Kanrin-maru

The *Kanrin-maru* was caught in a storm on its way to San Francisco. As a result, it took 37 days for the ship to reach its destination. This was the first time for Japanese to cross the Pacific on a ship steered by a Japanese.

In order to prevent possible collision between armies of the emperor and shogunate in and around the capital of Edo, Katsu Kaishū persuaded Saigō Takamori, staff officer of the emperor's army, to refrain from staging an all-out assault on the Edo Castle on condition that the shogunate army surrender the castle unconditionally.

Katsu Kaishū   Saigō Takamori

SAIGŌ TAKAMORI
西郷隆盛・1828—1877

One of the leaders of the Meiji Revolution. Son of a low-rank *samurai* of the Satsuma clan (Kagoshima Prefecture), Takamori saw the need of political revolution when he knew the wretched life of farmers of the day. He played a key role in the historic coalition between the Chōshū clan (Yamaguchi Prefecture) and the Satsuma clan, and in the peaceful surrender of the Edo Castle. Along with Sakamoto Ryōma, the manly Takamori was one of the heroic leaders of the Meiji Revolution.

The bronze statue of Saigō Takamori with his dog at Ueno is a symbol of the Ueno Park in Tōkyō.

When Takamori was appointed to army general by the Meiji government, he advocated the proposed Korean invasion as a means to relieve *samurai*s who had lost their jobs. As his opinion was rejected, he resigned from office and returned home in Kagoshima. There, supported by those *samurai*s who were discontented with the new government, he raised a rebellion against the Meiji government (Civil War of *Seinan*). Defeated in the war, he committed suicide, thereby putting an end to his eventful life.

SAKAMOTO RYŌMA
坂本龍馬・1836—1867

Patriot of the Tosa clan (Kochi Prefecture) who played a vital part in the Meiji Revolution. He considered it more important to modernize Japan than to pursue interest of his clan. A man of action and foresight, he was assassinated by a killer of the Tokugawa shogunate at the age of 31. As a hero of tragedy, he is very popular among many Japanese.

The following anecdote exemplifies Ryōma's foresight.

One day, Ryōma saw one of his friend wearing a long sword. Ryōma then showed his short sword to him and said, "Such a long sword is now of little use."

Another day, Ryōma saw the same friend carrying a short sword. Ryōma then took a pistol out his bosom and said, "You see, this is the latest weapon of Europeans."

Still other day, Ryōma saw that friend carrying a pistol. Ryōma then showed a book on international law to him and said, "The days of armed conflict are over."

As a child, Ryōma was often bullied into crying, hence called a crybaby. Besides, he was such a dull boy that his teacher almost abandoned hope of his improvement.

At the age of 13, Ryōma started practicing swordsmanship. As he improved his skill rapidly, his father had him enter a famous school of swordsmanship.

When Ryōma was 20 years of age, he obtained a detailed account of what was happening abroad from a painter named Kawada Shōryū. Deeply impressed by advanced European culture, he considered that in order to bring Japan up on the same level as Western countries, it was vitally necessary to reinforce Japan's naval force and foster talented personnel.

At the age of 26, Ryōma called on Katsu Kaishū, the then admiral of the shogunate, with the intention to kill him because Ryōma had thought that Kaishū was a traitor to his country. However, Ryōma shrank from his attempt at Kaishu's thundering cry, "Kill me after you hear my talk." Ryōma heard him talk and found many sympathies in common with him. Eventually, Ryōma became a pupil of Kaishū.

Kido Takayoshi　Ryōma　Saigō Takamori

When he was 29, Ryōma made strenuous efforts to attain coalition between the Satsuma clan (Kagoshima Prefecture) and the Chōshū clan (Yamaguchi Prefecture) which were the leading opponents to the shogunate. For example, he circulated some of the arms which the Satsuma clan had purchased through his trading firm at Nagasaki to the Choshu clan with a view to strengthening the tie between the two clans.

At last, Saigō Takamori of the Satsuma clan and Kido Takayoshi of the Chōshū clan agreed to When Ryōma found that either party was afraid of losing his face by breaking the ice about the coalition, he persuaded Saigō Takamori into giving way. The coalition between them was thus established.

At 30, Ryōma was attacked by a group of shogunate assassins while he was staying at an inn named *Teradaya* at Kyōto. On that occasion, he countered more than 20 killers firing his pistol. He could barely escape death then.

At the age of 31, Ryōma established a new organization called "Kaientai." This was a unique organization combining a shipping firm and naval force, whose purpose was to train personnel in linguistics and navigation, and thereby Ryōma aimed at realizing his long-cherished dream of building up a strong naval force and fostering talented personnel.

When one of the vessels of Kaientai sank after collision with a certain Japanese vessel, Ryōma proposed to the counterpart shipping company that the logbooks be exchanged and compensation for the damage be determined on the basis of international law. That was the first time for international law to be applied to a maritime accident within the boundary of Japan.

Japan must become modern nation!

Ryōma was also among those who made suggestions about the political system, such as the enactment of a constitution, amendment to treaties with foreign countries, and improvement of currency system, immediately after the shogunate was overthrown.

However, Ryōma could not witness the rejuvenated Japan. On November 15, 1867, he was assassinated in an inn at Kyōto, just before the Meiji Revolution was carried out.

KONDŌ ISAMI
近藤勇・1834—1868

Samurai of the late Edo period. As a vassal of the Tokugawa shogunate, he organized an armed force called *"Shinsen-gumi"* to oppress those who were aiming at the Meiji Restoration. Though the *Shinsen-gumi* wielded undisputed power in Kyōto for some time, Kondō Isami was eventually caught and beheaded by the imperial army.

The name "Kondō Isami" became widely known among later people thanks to the novel *"Kurama Tengu."* This is a story of a mysterious *samurai* named *"Kurama Tengu"* saving the lives of innovation-minded patriots from the bloodthirsty *Shinsen-gumi.*

Formerly, the *Shinsen-gumi* led by Kondō Isami was often treated in many novels and motion pictures as a group of villains opposed to Sakamoto Ryōma and other innovationists as the heroes. Recently, however, Kondō Isami and his followers began to be re-appraised as men who remained loyal to the Tokugawa shogunate to the last moment of its collapse.

Hijikata Toshizō

Okita Sōji

A master swordsman, who served as the righthand man of Kondō Isami. After the Meiji Restoration he continued to support the old *bakufu* forces, fighting against the new government in many battles around Japan. He eventually retreated to Hokkaidō, and when it became clear that his side would surrender in the final battle, he ended his life with a suicide-like death.

A member of the Shinsen-gumi, who was renowned as a peerless swordsman in his teens. Extremely handsome as well, he is said to have died a youthful death of tuberculosis, which has contributed to the legends associated with his name.

Ikeda-ya Incident

The most famous massacre by the *Shinsen-gumi*. Patriots of the Chōshū clan who led the innovationists concealed themselves in Kyōto and were planning to overthrow the shogunate even after they had been ordered to leave Kyōto. Therefore, they were the main target of the *Shinsen-gumi*. Becoming aware of the scheme of Chōshū clansmen to overthrow the shogunate, Kondō Isami and his 30 men raided on the *Ikeda-ya* inn where the innovationists were hiding themselves. There the *Shinsen-gumi* killed seven Chōshū clansmen and caught 23 others. This incident triggered off the *Kinmon* Incident in which the Chōshū clan fought with the Satsuma clan in Kyōto.

Great statesman of the Meiji period. After the Meiji Revolution, Itō Hirobumi displayed remarkable political talent in both internal and external affairs (the Constitution of Imperialist Japan was enacted by him). He became the first prime minister of Japan. Under the confidence of the Emperor Meiji, Hirobumi propelled modernization of Japan and opened the way for future prosperity.

Factory in London

Son of a low-rank *samurai* of the Chōshū clan, Ito Hirobumi went to England to study at the age of 21. There, he was impressed by their advanced industry and culture. When he returned home, he ardently advocated the open-door policy.

Winning the two wars (Sino-Japanese and Russo-Japanese), Japan seized the Korean peninsula and Itō Hirobumi was appointed to Resident-General of Korea. Eventually, he was shot to death by a young Korean who opposed to the Japanese-Korean amalgamation.

ITAGAKI TAISUKÉ
板垣退助・1837—1919

Statesman of the Meiji period. Leader of the campaign for democratic rights. Based on the belief that national power could be increased only by political involvement of the general public, he organized Japan's first political party (the Liberal Party) in 1881.

Itagaki Taisuké who played an active part in the battle against the Tokugawa shogunate was appointed to a high-rank office by the Meiji government. However, he lost his position when the Korean invasion he advocated together with Saigō Takamori was overruled. Thereafter, he promoted a movement for popularly elected assembly in the field.

In 1882, Itagaki Taisuké was stabbed in the chest by a ruffian in Gifu Prefecture. On that occasion, it is said, he cried, "Itagaki is dying, but liberty never dies!"

ŌKUMA SHIGENOBU
大隈重信・1838—1922

Statesman of the Meiji and Taishō periods. He displayed excellent ability in diplomatic and financial affairs. As the leader of the Constitutional Party, he organized Japan's first party cabinet. He was very popular among the general public, and his death was mourned by a grand nation-sponsored funeral service.

Waseda University

He is also known as the founder of Waseda University, one of Japan's most renowned universities. A statue of Ōkuma Shigenobu still stands on the campus of the university.

In 1888, Ōkuma Shigenobu, the then Foreign Minister, was attacked by a young rightist. The bomb thrown into Shigenobu's carriage exploded and blew off his right leg. Nevertheless, it is said that Shigenobu showed admirable composure to ask about the safety of his companions first.

FUKUZAWA YUKICHI
福沢諭吉・1835—1901

Enlightenment thinker of the Meiji period. From his childhood, he excelled in scholarship. He learned English without a master and was sent abroad by the shogunate to study modern civilization. He founded Keiō Gijuku University in 1868. Since then, he engaged himself in writing books advocating people's independence and abolishment of the traditional class system.

A portrait of Fukuzawa Yukichi is used on the current 10,000-yen note.

Keio Gijuku University

Keiō Gijuku University is a renowned private institution rivaled only by Waseda University.

While he was teaching pupils at his private school at Edo, a collision between the government and shogunate forces broke out nearby. Though the pupils were agitated, he did not stop giving lessons telling them, "No matter what may happen, I will not stop learning."

In his work "An Exhortation Toward Learning," he writes, "All men are equal under the sun." That was the first writing that introduced the equality of human right to the Japanese.

INUKAI TSUYOSHI
犬養毅・1855—1932

Statesman of the early Shōwa period. As prime minister, he endeavored to settle the Manchurian Incident (Sino-Japanese war) However, as he attempted to suppress the voice of the military, he was assassinated by a group of young military officers. Thereafter, the Japanese politics became increasingly militaristic and the country moved headlong toward the Second World War.

When young, he attended Keiō Gijuku University while serving on a newspaper. He started his political career when he was introduced to Ōkuma Shigenobu by Fukuzawa Yukichi who recognized his political talent.

On May 15, 1932, a group of eight young officers intruded upon Inukai's official residence. Inukai said to the intruders, "Let's talk together." "No use of discussion!" was their answer. He was shot to death on the spot.

158

YOSHIDA SHIGERU
吉田茂・1878—1967

Statesman who flourished during and after World War II. During the war, he was oppressed by the military for his pro-British and pro-American learnings. After the war, he strived to restore the devastated Japan in cooperation with General MacArthur of the occupation forces. From 1946 till 1954, as Prime Minister of postwar Japan, he implemented a number of drastic policies to regain the former vigor and prosperity of the country. Thus he was the foremost statesman symbolizing the recovery of postwar Japan.

At one time, he dashed a cup of water upon a newsman who displeased him.

The most brilliant achievement of Yoshida was that he signed the San Francisco Peace Treaty in 1951 and thereby brought Japan back to a member of international society.

Bakayarō!

Mad at a spiteful question from a member of the opposition party, Prime Minister Yoshida cried at him, "You fool!" This remark eventually forced Yoshida to dissolve the Diet.

Because of his obstinacy in character, Yoshida was called a 'one-man' prime minister.

Novelist and critic of the Meiji period. After he graduated from a university, he became a junior high school teacher, studied in England, and then became a lecturer at Tōkyō University. His humorous novel "I Am a Cat," of which a cat is the hero, brought him immediate fame. He originated his own world of literature characterized by modern individualism, and released in succession a number of works casting intense light upon the uneasiness of modern self and egoism. His contribution to the history of Japanese literature has been enormous.

He was born of a reputable family of Edo, but he led a wretched life in his childhood as the Meiji Restoration brought about the downfall of his family.

A portrait of Natsumé Sōseki is used in the current 1,000-yen note.

"I Am a Cat"
The novel which made Sōseki famous. He won a high reputation for a unique new plot of the novel, in which a nameless cat kept in the house of a junior high school teacher critically observes strange aspects of human society.

MORI ŌGAI
森鷗外・1862—1922

Novelist of the Meiji period. Along with Natsumé Sōseki, Mori Ōgai was the foremost figure of modern Japanese literature. In 1881, he graduated from the Medical Department of Tōkyō University at the age of 19 (the youngest graduate ever). While serving as an army surgeon, he released a number of works full of Romanticist flavor. He was one of the most notable intellectuals of the Meiji era who sought harmony and compromise between the traditional and the modern and between the conservative and the innovative.

He served as an army surgeon in the Sino-Japanese War. Eventually, he rose to the top post of Surgeon-General. It is said that he was always in military uniform even when he was at home.

Anju

Zushiō

"Sanshō Dayū"

One of Ōgai's masterpieces. This novel based on a legend of medieval Japan depicts in a splendid style the pitiful fate of two young heroes, Anju and Zushiō, sold to a slave-dealer.

ISHIKAWA TAKUBOKU
石川啄木・1885—1912

Poet of the late Meiji period. Born in Iwate Prefecture, he continued to write poems while serving as a part-time teacher of a primary school in the locality. Eventually, he came up to Tōkyō in search of a literary career. Unfortunately, he died of tuberculosis at the age of 37. Of many of his poems, those which lay bare his miserable heart amid poverty-stricken life are especially superb. In his latter years, he leaned toward socialistic thought.

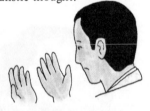

Here's one of his most famous poems:
"I've worked harder than hardest,
    Yet I'm no better off;
I only look down at my bony hands."

His life in Tōkyō (he had left his poor because his novels did not sell at all. When he found a job as proofreader at a newspaper office, he called his wife and children to Tokyo. However, their life became no better. Eventually, they all developed tuberculosis. Many of Takuboku's works were, therefore, characterized by his agony of poverty.

MIYAZAWA KENJI

宮沢賢治・1896—1933

Poet and fairy-tale writer of the early Shōwa period. While teaching at an agricultural school in Iwate Prefecture, he released original poems and fairy tales successively. He was affected by a serious illness at the age of 34. Thereafter, he spent most of his time in bed. It was only after his death that his works reflecting his sensibility as fragile as glassworks, his dreams in his boyhood, and his disappointment in real life came to be highly rated.

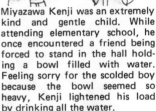

Miyazawa Kenji was an extremely kind and gentle child. While attending elementary school, he once encountered a friend being forced to stand in the hall holding a bowl filled with water. Feeling sorry for the scolded boy because the bowl seemed so heavy, Kenji lightened his load by drinking all the water.

"Kaze-no-Matasaburō"
One of the most famous fairy tales written by Miyazawa Kenji. He depicts in a fresh style a heartwarming interaction between an eccentric boy who came to a school in a remote village and schoolboys of the village.

KAWABATA YASUNARI
川端康成・1899—1972

Foremost novelist of modern Japan. He created his own world of Japanese aesthetics by expressing delicate changes in emotions of the characters and clear poetical sentiment through a keen eye of observation. He won a Nobel Prize for Literature in 1968. He committed suicide at the age of 73.

"Izu-no-Odoriko"
Yasunari's early masterpiece. This is a love story of a lonely student and a young dancer of an itinerant company whom he meets while traveling around Izu. This novel full of poetical sentiment has been brought to the screen several times, attracting much audience each time.

Snow Country

"Yukiguni"
One of Yasunari's supreme works. This is a story of fruitless love between a man tired of life and a *geisha* girl with a snowbound spa as the scene. Each of the elegant sentences represents exquisite beauty of the Japanese language.

MISHIMA YUKIO
三島由紀夫・1925—1970

Novelist who led off modern Japanese literature. In his notable work *"Kinkaku-ji"* and several others that followed, Mishima made an attempt to create his own aesthetic space. Thereafter, he leaned toward racialism and at the age of 45 he killled himself in a shocking way. His life was brought to the screen by Paul Schrader (titled *"Mishima"*). He is well-known both at home and abroad.

Mishima formed a right-wing organization called *"Tate-no-kai"* in 1968. In 1970, he led his followers into the Self-Defence Force Ichigaya Base. As his attempted coup d'etat failed, Mishima committed *hara-kiri* and was beheaded by one of his followers. The motive of this unusual action of Mishima has not been clarified to date.

"Kinkaku-ji"
One of Mishima's masterpieces whose theme was taken from the arson of Kinkaku-ji Temple at Kyōto in 1950. Mishima describes with overwhelming dynamism the psychological process of a young priest fascinated by the beauty of Kinkaku-ji Temple finding ultimate beauty in "Kinkaku-ji in flames" and eventually setting fire on the Temple with a view to materializing his image of ultimate beauty.

YOKOYAMA TAIKAN

横山大観・1868—1958

Master of modern Japanese painting. One of the founders of Japan Art Academy, Yokoyama Taikan had led the Japanese painting circles for 45 years since 1913. In the early period, he preferred color paintings. In and after the middle period, however, he opened a new world of Oriental idealism by black-and-white paintings.

"Inten," exhibit held by Japan Art Academy, has been the gateway to success for students of Japanese paintings.

One of Taikan's masterpieces *"Muga"* (Self-effacement)

KURODA SEIKI
黒田清輝・1866—1924

Artist of Western painting of the Meiji/Taisho periods. At the age of 18, Kuroda went to France and made himself famous as an artist. After his return home, he made efforts to popularize Western paintings in Japan. Since he preferred neutral tints of purple, his style was called "Purple school."

Kuroda's masterpiece "Reading"

Kuroda Seiki went to France with a view to studying French law. It is said, however, that he changed his mind when he was fascinated by the beauty of Western paintings as he accompanied his friend student of art to his atelier several times.

167

Educator of the Meiji period. Founder of *Kōdōkan* school of *jūdō*, Kanō Jigorō made efforts to spread *jūdō*. He is generally regarded as the father of Japanese gymnastics. In 1909, he was appointed as a member of the International Olympics Committee for the first time in Asia. At the IOC meeting held in Cairo in 1938, he succeeded in inviting the Olympics to Tōkyō. On his way home, however, he died of illness aboard the ship.

Present-day *Kōdōkan* at Bunkyō Ward, Tōkyō

When Kanō Jigorō began to teach *jūdō* at a certain university, he opened a *jūdō* hall at a corner of the temple where he lived in lodgings. In the hall which he named *"Kōdōkan,"* he taught English and Chinese literature, as well as *jūdō*. He regarded *jūdō* as an educational means to train the mind and body of human being.

RIKIDŌZAN
力道山・1924—1963

Professional wrestler who flourished in the 1950's. Formerly a *sumō* wrestler, Rikidōzan was a strong fighter with *'karate chop'* as his decisive trick. The time he flourished coincided with the period in which telecasting began spreading in Japan. Therefore, on the days when his match was telecasted, the TV sets installed at street corners gathered a large crowd of people.

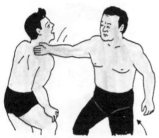

The black tights were the trade-mark of Rikidōzan.

Rikidōzan was stabbed in the abdomen by a young gangster and died in the hospital. It is said that the direct cause of his death was peritonitis he invited by drinking the water in a near-by flower-vase to relieve his thirst after the operation.

The secret of Rikidōzan's popularity was a morality play he introduced into professional wrestling, in which Rikidōzan, the hero, defeated a foreigner wrestler as the villain. He was, in a sense, symbolic of the re-juvenated Japan which just recovered from the shock of the defeat in the last war and was about to head for high growth economy.

OZU YASUJIRŌ
小津安二郎・1903—1963

Film director of the early Shōwa period. Along with Mizoguchi Kenji and Kurosawa Akira, Ozu Ysujirō is wellknown both at home and abroad. In the early period, he produced light comedies dealing mainly with modern morals. After World War II, he created his own world of film art by expressing delicate changes in human relationship of medium-level homes with plain touches.

Hara Setsuko
An exceptionally beautiful actress who played the leading part in many of Ozu's works, such as "Tōkyō Story."

Ozu Ysujirō was known as a perfectionist. It is said that he used to give his actors and actresses instructions in great detail — even the holding position of a cup. His works were characterized by low camera angles: the camera was never set above the eye level of actors.

NITOBÉ INAZŌ
新渡戸稲造・1862—1933

Educator of the Meiji and Taishō periods. He learned at Sapporo Agricultural School under Dr. Clark, American educator. After he studied in the United States and Germany, he taught at Tokyo University and Tokyo Women's University. He became Assistant Secretary-General of the Secretariat of the League of Nations in 1920. He is also known as the author of "Bushido" which explains the traditional principles of morality of the Japanese.

A portrait of Nitobe Inazō is used on the current 5,000-yen note.

As a cosmopolitan, Nitobe has left his footprints in various countries around the world. In Vancouver, Canada, where he died, there is a Japanese-style garden named "Nitobe Garden" in memory of his achievements there.

When Dr. Clark left Sapporo Agricultural School, he addressed to the students "Boys, be ambitious." At this remark in mind, Nitobe was determined to become an intermediary between the United States and Japan.

171

KITAZATO SHIBASABURŌ
北里柴三郎・1852—1931

Notable bacteriologist. While studying in Germany under Dr. Robert Koch, Kitazato grew the tetanus bacillus in pure culture and originated serum treatment. After he returned home, he established Kitazato Laboratory and made efforts to improve public health. Thus he made great contributions to the progress of modern Japanese medicine.

Dr. Koch

Kitazato was such an industrious person that he never left the most trifling question unsolved. Dr. Koch said, "Few of us Germans are so industrious as Kitazato."

Kitazato became director of Japan's first institute for research in infectious diseases. However, when that institute was made an annex to Tōkyō University, he resigned from his post saying that the mission of an institute could not be fulfilled when it became an annex to a university. Instead, he founded his own laboratory and brought up many talented scholars.

YUKAWA HIDEKI
湯川秀樹・1907—1981

Nuclear physicist. Yukawa predicted the existence of mesons and developed his theory on meson. For his work he won the Nobel Prize for physics in 1949, becoming the first Japanese to receive a Nobel award. In his latter years, he played a leading role in Japan's Peace Movement as a member of the "Seven-member Committee for Promotion of World Peace."

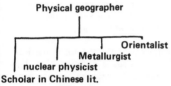

Physical geographer

Orientalist

Metallurgist

nuclear physicist

Scholar in Chinese lit.

The third son of a notable physical geographer, he took it for granted that he should become a scholar. His three brothers (metallurgist, Orientalist, Scholar in Chinese literature, respectively) have left a lot of remarkable achievements.

At first, Yukawa wanted to become a mathematician. It is said, however, that he abandoned that idea as a highschooler when the teacher in mathematics did not accept Yukawa's original method of proving mathematical theorems.

GLOSSARY

* Asuka Period (592 — 710) 飛鳥時代
The age when the capital was located in the Asuka region (Nara Prefecture), characterized by the establishment of a political system focused on the Emperor.

* Azuchi-Momoyama Period (1573 — 1602) 安土桃山時代
The era of rule by Oda Nobunaga (see page 74) and Toyotomi Hideyoshi (see page 78), two men who helped reunite Japan and bring an end to the "Age of Warring States." The name stems from the location of Oda's residential castle in Azuchi (Shiga Prefecture) and Toyotomi's castle in Momoyama (Kyoto). A short but crucial age in Japanese history, marked by the transition from the middle ages into the pre-modern ages.

* Daimyō 大名
Refers generally to samurai retainers of the shōgun in the Edo period, who were ordered to unify and rule a specific region. The term originated in the Heian period to describe regional land barons.

* Edo Period (1602 — 1867) 江戸時代
The age of rule by the Edo Bakufu (the generals of the Tokugawa family). The "closed country" policy of this period isolated Japan from international contact, leaving it far behind the rest of the world in terms of modernization. Positive aspects of the Edo period included the prolonged nationwide peace, and the flourishing of the kabuki theater, ukiyoé ("floating world painting") woodblocks, and other indigenous Japanese art and culture.

* Hatamoto 旗本
The samurai who had a revenue direct from the shogunate. It is said that hatamoto, including lower-level vassals, numbered some 80,000 – the strongest military corps in those days.

* Heian Period (794 — 1192) 平安時代
The age when the capital was located in Heian-kyō (Kyōto), with rule by the aristocrats, primarily the Fujiwara family. A period marked by the birth of a rich and splendid cultural heritage.

* Ikkō-shu Sect 一向宗
A separate name for the Pure Land Sect of Buddhism founded

by Shinran (see page 52). Revolts by sect followers (known as ikkō-ikki in Japanese) grew more frequent during the Age of Warring States. Inspired by their beliefs, the Buddhist hordes knew no fear of death, and the scale and intensity of the fighting was a source of considerable distress for the daimyō of that age.

* Jōruri 浄瑠璃

A traditional type of Japanese song, in which historical sagas are sung in ballad form by itinerant minstrels. The popularity of this entertainment spread far and wide, and in the Edo period a version sung in combination with a puppet theater also surfaces — a form which continues to be enjoyed today.

* Kabuki 歌舞伎

The kabuki theater claims its origins in the kabuki odori ("kabuki dancing') made popular in Kyōto during the end of the Age of Warring States by an all-female troupe led by Izumo-no-Okuni (see page 88). The word "kabuki" refers to something outlandish and vulgar in nature, and the kabuki odori was apparently considered an extremely decadent form of popular entertainment. The establishment of kabuki in its present form (spectacular theatrical performances by all-male casts) dates from the Edo period.

* Kamakura Period (1192 — 1333) 鎌倉時代

Japan's first genuine military government, during which the Kamakura Bakufu (shogunate) ruled the land. The name was taken from the capital city of Kamakura (Kanagawa Prefecture). This government was established by Minamoto-no-Yoritomo, although his descendants (the Genji Family) died out after only three generations. After that, the Hōjō Family (the descendants of Yoritomo's wife's family) took over the rule.

* Kojiki 古事記

Japan's first written historical account (containing a heavy mix of mythology), compiled at the beginning of the 8th century. The work,begins with the creation of the universe by Amaterasu-ōmikami (the god of the sun clamied to be the ancestor of the Emperor), and goes on to present an extended collection of myths and legends. It was compiled to give legitimacy to unification of the nation around the Emperor, but is also of extremely high ethnological value as Japan's oldest written document.

* Kyōgen 狂言

A classical Japanese art form, created in the middle ages from a combination of Japanese comic entertainment preserved from ancient times and a type of mime introduced from China. In the early days it was known as sarugaku, one form of which was further developed into Noh drama by Zeami (see page 62) in the Muromachi period. A separate version retaining a strong comic orientation came to be known as kyōgen, and continues to be enjoyed as amusing interludes for Noh plays today.

* Manyōshū 万葉集

Literally translated as "The Collection of a Thousand Leaves," the Manyōshū is the Japan's oldest anthology (see page 20).

* Meiji Period (1867 — 1912) 明治時代

The years which saw the collapse of the Edo shogunate, and the restoration of imperial rule within a new political system targeting national modernization. Chronologically, the period refers to the reign of the Meiji Emperor.

* Meiji Restoration 明治維新

The 1867 transfer of government power from the Edo shogunate to the Meiji Emperor, as Japan moved into the modern era.

* Muromachi Period (1394 — 1573) 室町時代

The age of rule by the Muromachi Bakufu, a shogunate established by the Ashikaga Family. The name stems from the residence of the shogun in the Muromachi district of Kyōto. With the collapse of the Kamakura Bakufu in 1336, political power fell into the hands of Ashikaga Takauji (see page 58). In official historical terms, however, the Muromachi period begins from the uniting of the North and South Courts. The authority of the Muromachi Bakufu plummeted after the Ōnin Revolt of 1467, with the subsequent period known as the "Age of Warring States" (Sengoku Jidai).

* Nara Period (710 — 784) 奈良時代

The brief age when the capital city was Nara. Highlights include the designation of Buddhism as a state religion, and the establishment of Buddhist temples and images throughout Japan.

＊Southern and Northern Courts (1336 – 1394) 南北朝時代
A period characterized by two separate imperial courts – the Southern Court of the Emperor Godaigo in Yoshino (Nara Prefecture), and the Northern Court in Kyōto backed by Ashikaga Takauji (see page 58). In reality, the Northern Court (a military government) maintained absolute superiority, with the Southern Court failing to ever seize the reigns of power.

＊Sankin-kōtai 参勤交代
The system in which all feudal lords were required to attend the shogun's court at Edo (later Tokyo) in alternate years to guard the capital of Edo. The purpose of this system was to have them spend considerable amounts of money so as to prevent them from amassing sinews of rebellion against the shogunate.

＊Sengoku Daimyō (Warring State Land Barons) 戦国大名
The loss of sovereign power by the Muromachi Bakufu marked the beginning of the "Age of Warring States," during which the regional daimyō (land barons) assumed absolute control over their own fiefs. These land barons are referred to as sengoku daimyō to distinguish them from the daimyō of the Edo period, who were the loyal retainers of the all-powerful shōgun(generalissimo).

＊Sengoku Jidai ("Age of Warring States") 戦国時代
The part of the Muromachi period lasting from the Ōnin Revolt of 1467 (when the Muromachi Bakufu fell out of power) through the reuniting of Japan by Nobunaga Oda (see page 74) during which individual sengoku daimyō warlords battled each other for control.

＊Sesshō (Regent) 摂政
An official in charge of handling political affairs in place of a child or female Emperor. During the Heian period, however, the position of regent was used to seize control of the government, with emperor after emperor forced to retire around the age of 20, before assuming true powers.

* Shikken (Regent) 執権

A key post established in the Kamakura period as the No.2 man next to the shōgun, later inherited by the Hōjo clan, the family of the wife of Minamoto-no-Yoritomo(see page 42). The method of rule after the Hōjo family seized control of the Kamakura Bakufu is known as shikken seiji (rule by regency).

* Shōgun (Generalissimo) 将軍

The highest position attainable by a warrior (samurai). Shōgun was the name given to the commander-in-chief of military forces dispatched by imperial order in the Heian period. Under the military government which dominated Japan from the Kamakura period through the Edo period, however, the position of shōgun came to be synonymous with the ruler of Japan.

* Tennō (Emperor) 天皇

The position of "Emperor," still considered a major symbol of the Japanesenation, dates from the 7th century A.D , when the term was coined to refer to the head monarch of the Yamato Court. Historically, the Imperial family can be traced back to around the 4th century A.D., while Japanese mythology claims family lines dating as far back as 660 B.C..In either case, it is certainly Japan's oldest identifiable family, although its political position has varied widely from age to age.

As regional monarchs working to unify the nation under the Yamato Court, the early emperors steadily increased their power, and in the Nara period were even considered the "rightful rulers of Japan for eternity" because of their supposed blood descent from the "god of the sun." By the Heian period, however, the Emperor was increasingly manipulated by the aristocrats who held the real political power, and in comparison to the family's religious (spiritual) authority, its political strength declined conspicuously. This trend became increasingly pronounced under the warrior class rule from the Kamakura through the Edo periods, with the only real significance of the Emperor coming to be as a symbol of the legitimacy of the military government. With the Meiji Restoration of 1867 Japan was transformed into a modern state, and the Emperor was once again placed at the zenith of political power. Up until World War II, he was considered by many to be a god, the father of all Japanese, and the Japanese nation and spirit itself. The rise of militarism took place in the midst of this Imperial system, and led to the Japanese invasion of China. As a result, the American forces which occupied Japan after its defeat quickly stripped the Emperor of all political authority (both real and supposed), and retained the position as a national symbol. This system continues today, and although all his political powers are gone, the Emperor continues to exert an incalculable spiritual impact over the Japanese people.

* Udaijin (Minister of the Right) 右大臣
An important post in the bureaucracy established in the Nara period (which placed the Emperor at the focus). It was the No.3 position in the hierarchy, after the so-called Dajōdaijin ("Prime Minister") and Sadaijin (Minister of the Left), but gradually lost all real authority in the Heian period as the government came to be ruled by regency.

* Yamatai Koku 邪馬台国
A regional nation believed to have been the political focus of Japan around the 3rd century, ruled by Queen Himiko. Because an envoy was sent to Gi China, written records of this age exist in China. However, there is no clear proof of the exact location of Yamatai Koku, with the controversy divided between two areas – Kyūshū (the main southern island) and Yamato (present-day Nara Prefecture).

* Yamato Court 大和朝廷
The ancestors of the Imperial Family. "Yamato" is the place name referring to what is today Nara Prefecture, and ranked as one of the most powerful regions in the 3rd to 4th centuries. The Court organized Japan as a national polity in the 5th to 6th century, established the aristocratic government (with the focus on the Emperor) which continued through the Asuka, Nara and Heian periods, and laid the foundation for the Imperial Family which continues to exist today.

• HISTORICAL TABLE

C.	Era	Year	Historical affairs
3	Yayoi and Yamato Periods	239	Queen Himiko of the *Yamatai-koku* dispatches envoy to Gi Dynasty of China.
			Yamato Court unites Japan.
5		413	Emperor Nintoku dispatches envoy to China.
			Shōtoku Taishi becomes *sesshō* (regent).
7	Asuka Period	607	Hōryū-ji Temple completed.
			Political system established with focus on Emperor.
8	Nara Period	710	National capital moved to Nara.
		752	Emperor Shōmu builds great image of Buddha in Nara.
		790	Man-yōshū anthology compiled (Kakinomoto-no-Hitomaro).
	Heian Period	794	National capital moved to Kyoto.
9		805	Saichō establishes Tendai-shū Sect of Buddhism.
		806	Kūkai establishes Shingon-shū Sect of Buddhism.
10		901	Sugawara-no-Michizané exiled to Kyūshū.
		939	Taira-no-Masakado leads rebellion.
11		1001	Sei-Shōnagon completes *Makura-no-Sōshi*.
		1011	Murasaki Shikibu completes *Genji Monogarari* ("The Tales of Genji").
		1017	Fujiwara-no-Michinaga becomes *Dajō-daijin* (leading Imperial advisor).
12		1156	The warrior class gains power with the *Hogen* Rebellion.
		1159	The *Heishi* clan defeats the *Genji* clan in the *Heiji* Rebellion.
		1167	Taira-no-Kiyomori becomes *Dajō-daijin*. Reign of the *Taira* clan reaches its peak.
		1175	Hōnen establishes *Jōdo-shū* Sect of Buddhism.

C.	Era	Year	Historical affairs
13	Kamakura Period	1180	Minamoto-no-Yoritomo gathers together forces to overthrow the *Taira* rule.
		1185	Minamoto-no-Yoshitsuné overthrows *Heishi* clan.
		1192	Minamoto-no-Yoritomo becomes *shōgun*, and establishes Shogunate in Kamakura.
		1203	The *Hōjo* family becomes *shikken* (regent advisor to the *shogun*), taking over the real power within the Shogunate.
		1224	Shinran establishes *Jōdoshin-shū* Sect of Buddhism.
		1253	Nichiren establishes *Nichiren-shū* Sect of Buddhism.
		1274	Mongol forces attack Japan, are repelled.
		1281	Mongols attack and are repelled again; power of Kamakura Shogunate weakened.
14	Southern and Northern Courts	1334	Emperor Godaigo overthrows Kamakura Shogunate restores imperial system.
		1336	Kusunoki Masashigé dies in battle. Ashikaga Takauji throws support behind Emperor in Kyōto (Northern Court), forcing Emperor Godaigo to retreat to Yoshino (Southern Court).
	Muromachi Period	1341	Ashikaga Takauji becomes *shōgun*.
		1392	Ashikaga Yoshimitsu unites Southern and Northern Courts.
		1397	Kinkaku-ji Temple (Golden Pavilion)
		1400	Zeami completes the *Kadansho* ("The Book of Noh theory").
15		1467	Battle of *Ōnin* (a large-scale rebellion centered in Kyoto) begins. Sesshū travels to China to study.

C.	Era	Year	Historical affairs
16		1477	Battle of Ōnin ends, Kyoto is reduced to ashes, and Sengoku period ("Age of Warring States") begins.
		1489	Ashikaga Yoshimasa completes the Ginkaku-ji Temple (Silver Pavilion).
		1491	Hōjo Sōun expands his family's land holdings.
		1543	Portuguese sailors introduce firearms to Japan.
		1549	Spanish missionaries arrive in Japan to spread the teaching of Christianity.
	Azuchi-Momoyama Period	1555	Takeda Shingen clashes with Uesugi Kenshin.
		1573	Oda Nobunaga overthrows the Muromachi Shogunate.
		1582	Oda Nobunaga is betrayed by a disloyal man and assassinated.
		1585	Toyotomi Hideyoshi defeats all formidable daimyō to succeed Oda.
		1598	Toyotomi Hideyoshi dies.
17	Edo Period	1600	Tokugawa Ieyasu defeats the forces of Toyotomi in the Battle of Sekigahara.
		1603	Tokugawa Ieyasu becomes shōgun, establishes Shogunate in Edo (present-day Tokyo). Izumo-no-Okuni begins to perform kabuki-odori ("Kabuki dancing") around this period.
		1615	Last remaining members of Toyotomi clan wiped out.
		1626	Christianity is banned in Japan.
		1637	Amakusa Shirō leads Shimabara Rebellion.
		1639	"Closed-country" policy implemented on full-scale bases.
		1682	Ihara Saikaku is active around this period.
		1687	Tokugawa Tsunayoshi becomes shōgun.
		1693	Matsuo Bashō writes Oku-no-Hosomichi.
18		1702	Ōishi Kuranosuké avenges the death of his lord.

C.	Era	Year	Historical affairs
19	Meiji Period	1715	Chikamatsu Monzaemon active around this period.
		1716	Tokugawa Yoshimune becomes *shōgun*.
		1774	Sugita Gempaku completes *Kaitai Shinsho*.
		1798	Motoori Norinaga completes *Kojiki-den*.
		1800	Inō Tadataka implements land survey of entire Japanese nation.
		1814	Takizawa Bakin completes *Nansō Satomi Hakkenden*.
		1853	U.S. gunboats commanded by Admiral Perry arrive in Japanese waters.
		1866	Sakamoto Ryōma organizes forces to oppose the Shogunate.
		1867	Tokugawa Yoshimunē becomes *shōgun,* turns over government control to the Meiji Emperor.
		1892	Fukuzawa Yukichi completes *Gakumon-no-Susumē*("Exhortation Toward Learning").
		1877	Saigō Takamori perishes in *Satsuma* Rebellion.
		1882	Ōkuma Shigenobu forms Progressive Party.
		1885	Itō Hirobumi becomes Japan's first prime minister.
		1889	The Imperial Constitution of Japan promulgated.
		1894	Sino-Japanese War fought.
20	Taisho Period Showa Period	1904	Russo-Japanese War fought.
		1910	Japanese annexation of Korea.
		1923	Tokyo region devastated by major earthquake.
		1932	Inukai Tsuyoshi assassinated.
		1941	Pacific War begins.
		1945	Hiroshima and Nagasaki suffer atomic attacks, Japan agrees to unchonditional surrender.
		1946	Yoshida Shigeru cabinet promulgates Constitution of Japan.
		1949	Yukawa Hideki receives Nobel Prize.

LIST OF NAMES (Family Name)

LIST OF NAMES (First Name)

I N D E X

952.048 W62w 1987

Who's who of Japan : 100
historical personages :

HAY LIBRARY
WESTERN WYOMING COMMUNITY COLLEGE

DEMCO